SERVING
FROM THE
HEART

SERVING FROM THE HEART

Faith-Driven Stories and Transformative Strategies for Servant Leadership and Lasting Impact

Tricia Andreassen
with Co-Authors Coni Meyers, Al Ferreira, Wendy Gunn, Natalie Martin, Jaclyn Michelle Nagle, Cindy Craig Hall, Garrett Milby, and Karen Storey

Creative Life Publishing
& Leadership Institute

Creative Life Publishing & Learning Institute

www.CLPLI.com
Info@CLPLI.com

Book Versions
Ingram ISBN: 978-1-946265-45-6
eBook ISBN: 978-1-946265-46-3
KDP Paperback ISBN: 978-1-946265-47-0
KDP Hardback ISBN: 978-1-946265-48-7

Copyright © 2025 Creative Life Publishing & Learning Institute All rights reserved. No part of this book may be reproduced in any form without prior written permission from the publisher. This work represents the views and opinions of the author alone. No liability in conjunction with the content or the use of ideas connected with this work is assumed by the publisher.

REALTOR® is a registered trademark.

THE HOLY BIBLE, NEW INTERNATIONAL VERSION®,

NIV® Copyright © 1973, 1978, 1984, 2011 by Biblica, Inc.® Used by permission. All rights reserved worldwide.

"New International Version" and "NIV" are registered trademarks of Biblica, Inc.®

CONTENTS

**Embracing the Spirit of Servant Leadership: | 1
A Journey of Inspiration**
By Tricia Andreassen

**Transformative Leadership: Creating Resilience | 23
Through Kickbutt Leadership and Servant
Leadership**
By Coni Meyers, LMC, CBLC, CDC

Practicing Servant Leadership Artisan | 37
By Alvaro "Al" Ferreira

Is Becoming A Servant Leader: My Journey | 51
By Wendy Gunn

You Are Created For Greatness | 67
By Natalie Martin

Reflecting on Life's Journey: Embracing a Legacy | 89
By Jaclyn Michelle Nagle

**Legacy of Leadership: The 5C Framework |103
for Serving Others**
By Cindy Craig Hall

People of Transformation | 123
By Garrett Milby

Servant Leadership in Education | 139
By Karen Storey

In the Eye of the Storm: | 151
A Journey of Servant Leadership
By Tricia Andreassen

EMBRACING THE SPIRIT OF SERVANT LEADERSHIP: A JOURNEY OF INSPIRATION

By Tricia Andreassen

EMBRACING THE SPIRIT OF SERVANT LEADERSHIP: A JOURNEY OF INSPIRATION

What defines a true leader? And, even deeper, a heart-centered servant leader?

In a world where leadership is often tied to authority and control, there is a deeper, more transformative path—one that doesn't rely on power but on uplifting others, even when we ourselves feel fragile. This is the heart of servant leadership: a choice that changes not only our own lives but also the lives of those we touch.

At its core, servant leadership is not about standing above others; it's about rising together. Yet, this path can be challenging. Life presents us with encounters that test our patience—whether it's dealing with someone in a bad mood or feeling judged by those who "size us up" in just a few seconds. It's in these moments that we're called to lean into something greater than ourselves, to show grace when grace is least expected.

I often reflect on the wisdom of my mentor, John Maxwell, who says, *"I choose for you not to be a stranger in this world. Instead, I choose to live my life by looking you in the eye and saying, 'Hi, I'm John Maxwell, and I'm your friend.'"*

Imagine a world where leaders aren't defined by titles but by the choices they make—choices rooted in empathy, compassion, and service. For those of us inspired by the teachings of Christ, servant leadership isn't just a strategy; it's a way of life. It's the embodiment of biblical principles like selflessness, encouragement, and unwavering love, even in a world that often feels harsh and unpredictable.

But let's be honest—this kind of leadership can feel counterintuitive. Why focus on serving when we're striving for success? The answer lies in what success truly means. If our goal is to stand one day before Jesus and account for the work we've done on Earth, then our greatest achievements won't be measured by power but by how we empowered others. Servant leadership builds trust and fosters collaboration, creating spaces where people feel valued, supported, and inspired to contribute their best.

For me, this journey has been deeply personal. It's about choosing to lead with an open heart, even when circumstances make it difficult. It's about recognizing that through every small act of service, we plant seeds of transformation that can grow into something far greater than ourselves.

At first glance, servant leadership might not seem like the obvious choice, especially when the world tells us to focus on climbing higher, achieving more, and taking charge. But when we pause to reflect, we realize that true fulfillment doesn't come from power—it comes from purpose. And our greatest purpose lies in the impact we have on others.

When we choose to serve, we create environments filled with trust, collaboration, and hope. These are spaces where people feel seen and heard, where their gifts are nurtured, and their potential is realized. In these moments, leadership becomes more than a role—it becomes a calling to uplift and empower.

I've witnessed this firsthand in my journey as an entrepreneur. For years, I poured my energy into building my publishing company, helping authors find their voices and share their stories with the world. I loved seeing their messages take shape and knowing that I played a part in equipping them to step onto stages and into the lives of those who needed their words. But life has a way of shifting our focus.

In June 2021, I faced a life-changing diagnosis that redirected my attention toward my own health. Countless doctor appointments, tests, and treatments consumed my days. I was in survival mode, focusing on the next step in managing my chronic pain and uncertainty. What I didn't realize was that, even in my absence, the seeds I had planted were continuing to grow.

Looking back now, I am amazed to see how those I once guided have flourished. Some have become speakers, sharing their stories on national platforms. Others have published books, created courses, and even stepped into roles in television and media. Their success is a testament to the power of servant leadership. When we invest in others—sharing our gifts, talents, and strengths with open hearts—God takes that investment and multiplies it in ways we can't imagine.

This is the beauty of servant leadership. It's not about us. It's about the legacy we create by lifting others up and helping them shine. Imagine what our world would look like if every leader—whether in a company, a classroom, or a family—chose to lead with this mindset.

My friend Coni who is an Author in this book, comes to mind, whose nonprofit helps children in crisis. Her passion and dedication inspire me deeply. Not only does she inspire me, but she has also been by my side through my best and worse times. She is my mentor, and she probably doesn't even realize it. She has become like family to me.

Then there's my sister, Karen, whose selfless love and leadership continue to guide and encourage me. Since I was born, she looked out for me. Fourteen years older than me she has always been there cheering me on even when we have both been challenged in our own relationship at times dealing with our own personal struggles of not feeling adequate. And through it all she serves me so fully. I never fully understood her deep desire of wanting to serve others so deeply until my own walk over the last ten years. In fact, as I write this, I am coming up on a ten-year anniversary of how these two women have been my anchor. They are the example of Servant Leaders that I strive to be. These women embody what it means to lead with purpose and heart, and they remind me that true leadership leaves an indelible mark on those we serve.

Every moment we spend as servant leaders presents us with a choice: to listen, to encourage, and to support those around us. It's in these simple yet powerful acts that we create a ripple effect—one that not only transforms the lives of those we lead but also transforms us. Humility becomes our greatest strength, not a weakness. It allows us to honor the unique contributions of others while fostering an environment where everyone feels valued.

Servant leadership is special because it transcends boundaries. It's not confined to corporate boardrooms or organizational hierarchies—it's a way of being that can be practiced anywhere. Whether at work, at home, or in the community, its principles can build stronger relationships and infuse every interaction with meaning and purpose.

That is why these folks who have decided to become Authors in this book are so powerful. From all walks of life, they are showing their own authenticity of what servant leadership means to them. They are giving us a glimpse into their own life so we can reflect into our own. I am humbled to be a part of it.

I invite you to join me on this journey as we explore the heart of servant leadership together. In the chapters ahead, we'll dive into the values and actions that define this approach—empathy, humility, and purposeful service—and discover how to put them into practice in every aspect of our lives. We'll examine how servant leadership can strengthen teams, deepen connections, and create environments where trust and collaboration thrive.

But more importantly, we'll explore how choosing to lead through service transforms us. When we prioritize others, we find deeper fulfillment. When we empower others to shine, we discover our greatest successes. And when we build a legacy rooted in kindness and love, we leave the world better than we found it.

This is the heart of servant leadership. It's not about power, position, or prestige. It's about building something greater than we—communities defined by strength, unity, and care.

Putting Servant Leadership into Action
Living out the principles of servant leadership in our daily lives can feel both rewarding and challenging. It requires intentionality, perseverance, and a willingness to step outside of our comfort zones. But when we embrace this calling, the impact is undeniable—not just in the lives of others but in our own growth as well.

In my journey as an entrepreneur, servant leadership has been a guiding force. Here's how I strive to embody these principles in both my personal and professional life:

1. Empowering Others to Lead

A pivotal part of servant leadership is recognizing and fostering leadership qualities in others. It's not about holding all the power or being the one with all the answers—it's about sharing the spotlight and equipping others to step into their own potential.

For me, this means delegating meaningful tasks and responsibilities, trusting that others can rise to the occasion. When we create opportunities for people to grow, we not only strengthen them but also build a foundation of collaboration and shared vision.

This principle extends beyond the workplace. At home, I draw inspiration from the example of Jesus' leadership, striving to create an environment where love, respect, and communication flourish. Whether as a wife, mother, or friend, I want to nurture spaces where those I care about feel supported and encouraged to become their best selves.

2. Modeling Love and Service

Servant leadership begins with action. It's not enough to talk about service—we must live it. Whether it's volunteering at a local food bank, creating art that inspires hope, or giving small gifts to brighten someone's day, these acts are tangible expressions of love and compassion.

These moments remind us of the joy that comes from giving back. They also plant seeds of kindness in the hearts of others, creating a ripple effect that mirrors the selflessness taught by Jesus. Service isn't just about helping others; it's about cultivating empathetic hearts and showing the world what it means to live with purpose and intention.

3. Prioritizing People Over Profits

In business, success is often measured by numbers—revenue, growth, and market share. But servant leadership challenges us to look deeper. It calls us to prioritize people over profits, creating environments where individuals feel valued, empowered, and motivated to contribute their best.

This could mean offering flexible work schedules, investing in personal development, or fostering team-building activities that emphasize collaboration and community impact. By placing people at the center, we cultivate not only productivity but also loyalty, trust, and long-term success.

4. Encouraging Open Communication

Trust is the foundation of any successful relationship, whether in business, at home, or within a community. As servant leaders, we create environments where communication is transparent, honest, and rooted in mutual respect. This means actively listening—not just hearing words, but truly understanding the emotions, needs, and aspirations behind them.

In my journey, I've learned the value of creating safe spaces where people feel empowered to share their thoughts without fear of judgment. When feedback is welcomed and concerns are addressed with sincerity, we cultivate relationships built on trust and integrity.

In practice, this could look like:

- Hosting team meetings where every voice is heard, and ideas are valued.
- Sitting down with a loved one to listen, fully present, to their challenges and dreams.
- Offering a kind word or encouragement to someone who might be struggling silently.

Open communication fosters connection, strengthens relationships, and paves the way for collaboration. It reminds others that they matter, and that their contributions—no matter how small—are essential.

5. Embracing Empathy in Everyday Interactions

Empathy is at the heart of servant leadership. It's the ability to step into someone else's shoes, to see the world through their eyes, and to respond with compassion. When we lead with empathy, we create spaces where people feel seen, heard, and valued.

As a business leader, I've found that empathy transforms workplace dynamics. It builds morale, trust, and cooperation, fueling a culture where people feel supported and motivated to bring their best selves to the table. But empathy doesn't stop at the office door—it extends to our families, friends, and communities.

In daily life, embracing empathy can look like:

- Taking time to understand a colleague's challenges before offering solutions.

- Recognizing the emotions behind a child's frustration and responding with patience and love.
- Offering grace to someone who may be acting out of pain or stress.

When we practice empathy, we not only nurture stronger connections but also inspire others to do the same, creating a ripple effect of kindness and understanding.

6. Encouraging Growth and Development

As servant leaders, one of our greatest responsibilities is to help others grow—both personally and professionally. This means investing in their development, celebrating their successes, and supporting them through failures.

In business, this could involve offering training opportunities, mentoring team members, or encouraging creative problem-solving. At home, it might mean guiding loved ones toward their goals, cheering them on as they step into new challenges, and teaching resilience through shared experiences.

For me, there is no greater joy than seeing the people I've mentored go on to achieve incredible things. Whether it's an author I've helped publish their first book or a leader I've encouraged to step onto a stage, their success is a testament to the power of empowerment.

In every setting, fostering growth looks like:

- Creating opportunities for learning and skill-building.
- Supporting others in exploring their passions and stepping outside their comfort zones.

- Celebrating milestones and viewing setbacks as opportunities for growth.

When we invest in the growth of others, we create legacies of transformation. We multiply our impact by empowering others to carry their own torch and light the way for even more people.

Overcoming Challenges in Adopting Servant Leadership

While the rewards of servant leadership are profound, embracing this approach isn't without its challenges. It often requires a significant mindset shift, especially in a world that frequently prioritizes control, authority, and results above all else.

One of the greatest hurdles is overcoming the traditional top-down leadership model. Many organizations—and even individuals—are accustomed to equating leadership with power. Servant leadership, by contrast, calls us to relinquish the need for control and instead focus on empowering others. This can feel counterintuitive, especially when faced with the pressure to deliver results quickly.

Another challenge is vulnerability. Serving others with humility often means stepping outside of our comfort zones, admitting when we don't have all the answers, and being willing to share in both triumphs and failures. It requires a level of authenticity that can feel uncomfortable, especially in environments where leaders are expected to appear infallible.

Despite these challenges, the rewards far outweigh the difficulties. When we choose servant leadership, we build trust, foster collaboration, and create spaces where innovation and resilience thrive. Overcoming these obstacles begins with a commitment to growth—both for ourselves and those we lead.

Cultivating a Servant Leader Mindset

Servant leadership isn't just a style—it's a way of life. It requires intentionality, self-reflection, and a deep commitment to prioritizing others. Here's how to cultivate this mindset:

1. Practice Mindfulness and Reflection

Regular self-reflection is key to aligning your actions with the principles of servant leadership. Take time to evaluate your values, motivations, and decisions. Are they rooted in empathy and service? Are they building others up? Mindfulness can also enhance your emotional intelligence, allowing you to respond with greater compassion and understanding in challenging situations.

2. Build Genuine Relationships

At the heart of servant leadership is a genuine interest in the well-being of others. Invest in relationships by taking the time to understand people's goals, challenges, and unique contributions. These connections create a foundation of trust and collaboration, allowing teams—and families—to thrive.

3. Commit to Lifelong Learning

A servant leader is always growing. Whether through personal development, professional training, or spiritual growth, make a commitment to continuous learning. This not only enhances your ability to lead but also sets an example for others to embrace growth in their own lives.

4. Embrace Flexibility and Adaptability

The journey of servant leadership often requires us to pivot and adapt. It means being open to new ideas, listening to feedback, and recognizing when a change in direction is needed. This willingness to evolve ensures that we remain effective and relevant in an ever-changing world.

5. Lead with Love and Vision

Servant leadership calls us to lead with love—a love that is patient, kind, and selfless. Pair this love with a clear vision of what's possible when people come together in unity and purpose. As servant leaders, we are not just guiding others—we're inspiring them to dream bigger, reach higher, and believe in what they can achieve.

The Heart of a Servant Leader

The journey of servant leadership is transformative, rooted in humility, empathy, and a genuine desire to see others succeed. It challenges us to look beyond our own goals and focus on the greater good. It reminds us that leadership isn't about titles or power—it's about the legacy we create by serving others.

By adopting this mindset, we can foster environments where innovation thrives, teams develop resilience, and success is shared by all. More importantly, we create ripples of kindness and purpose that extend far beyond ourselves, leaving the world a better place for generations to come.

The path of servant leadership is not always easy, but it is always worth it. And as we walk this path together, we can build something truly extraordinary—a life, a business, and a community rooted in love, service, and unstoppable impact.

The Positive Impacts of Servant Leadership

Servant leadership doesn't just transform individuals—it has the power to reshape organizations, families, and entire communities. When leaders prioritize service, they cultivate cultures of trust, collaboration, and shared purpose. These environments don't just feel better to be a part of; they also produce tangible results.

Consider the example of Southwest Airlines. Their culture of servant leadership has been a cornerstone of their success. By empowering employees to act with honesty, creativity, and a focus on customer needs, they've created a workplace where people are motivated and engaged. This ethos doesn't just benefit the employees—it's reflected in the loyalty of their customers and the strength of their brand.

Now, imagine applying this same principle on a smaller scale—in your family, your business, or your community. Servant leadership can manifest in countless ways, such as:

- Encouraging a colleague to take the lead on a project and offering support along the way.
- Prioritizing quality time with family members to strengthen relationships and foster open communication.
- Volunteering for a cause that aligns with your values, inspiring others to join you in making a difference.

Every act of service, no matter how small, creates a ripple effect. It reminds people of their worth, encourages them to step into their potential, and inspires them to pay it forward.

Overcoming Resistance to Servant Leadership

Adopting a servant leadership approach isn't always met with immediate understanding or acceptance. Some may view it as too "soft" or impractical in fast-paced, results-driven environments. However, the key to overcoming resistance lies in demonstrating the results—not just through words but through actions.

For example:

- Show how prioritizing employee well-being leads to higher engagement and retention.
- Share stories of how serving others has led to unexpected opportunities and growth.
- Be consistent in your approach, even when faced with skepticism. Over time, your commitment to servant leadership will build trust and inspire others to follow suit.

Remember, servant leadership isn't about proving others wrong—it's about staying true to your values and letting the results speak for themselves.

Moving Forward: Steps to Embody Servant Leadership

If you're ready to embrace servant leadership, here are practical steps to begin your journey:

1. **Reflect on Your "Why"**: Take time to consider why servant leadership resonates with you. What motivates you to serve others? What legacy do you want to leave behind?

2. **Start Small**: You don't need to overhaul your life overnight. Begin with small acts of service, like offering encouragement, helping a colleague, or volunteering your time.

3. **Listen and Learn**: Cultivate the habit of listening—really listening—to others. Understand their needs, aspirations, and challenges. Let this understanding guide your actions.

4. **Empower Others**: Look for opportunities to uplift those around you. Delegate meaningful tasks, celebrate their successes, and support their growth.

5. **Lead by Example**: Your actions will always speak louder than your words. Be consistent in your commitment to servant leadership, and let your life be a testimony to its power.

6. **Stay Rooted in Faith and Values**: For me, the teachings of Christ provide a constant reminder of what it means to lead with love, humility, and purpose. Find what anchors you and let it guide your journey.

Becoming an Instrument of Change

Servant leadership isn't just a method—it's a movement. It's a choice to live with purpose, to lead with love, and to leave the world better than we found it.

As you step into this calling, know that your actions have the power to create ripples of transformation. Each act of service, no matter how small, contributes to a legacy of compassion, strength, and unity. Together, we can build communities defined not by competition but by collaboration—not by power but by empowerment.

Let's walk this path together, choosing every day to lead by serving, to love without limits, and to live a life that inspires others to do the same.

Servant Leadership Reflections

1. **Reflect on a time when you chose to serve rather than lead with authority.**

   What motivated your decision, and what impact did it have on others? How did it make you feel about your role as a leader?

   _____
   _____
   _____
   _____
   _____
   _____

2. **What does the phrase "empowering others to lead" mean to you?**

   Identify one person in your life—whether at work, home, or in your community—that you can support in stepping into their leadership potential. What steps can you take to help them grow?

   _____
   _____
   _____
   _____
   _____
   _____

3. **Consider how you handle challenges that test your patience and humility as a leader.**

   How do you typically respond to criticism, rejection, or moments when others seem to misunderstand you?

   _____
   _____
   _____
   _____
   _____

4. **Imagine the impact you want to have on the lives of those you lead. What is one action you want to take today to build that legacy?**

   _____
   _____
   _____
   _____
   _____

5. **What legacy of servant leadership do you want to leave behind?**

   _____
   _____
   _____
   _____
   _____

AUTHOR BIOGRAPHY

Tricia Andreassen

From a young age, Tricia Andreassen knew her calling was to inspire and bring hope to audiences worldwide as a speaker and singer. At just 19 years old, she became an entrepreneur by purchasing her first real estate property with no money in her pocket, growing up in a trailer. Her passion for business ignited when she took her first Marketing and Economics classes and becoming an assistant for a real estate broker while being mentored from a prominent attorney. After the tragic loss of a close friend in a car accident, Tricia channeled her grief into writing a heartfelt story of hope, which she sent to the grieving mother. Encouraged by her English professor, who mentored her writing, Tricia began to align her talents and life purpose.

If you have ever felt you were meant for more in your life and believe that your business and personal purpose can harmoniously blend, Tricia's message is for you. Or, if you've already built your business and grown your influence. Now, it's time to share that expertise with the world.

With over 30 years of experience, Tricia Andreassen has mastered the art of transforming knowledge into powerful, impactful communication. She has shared the stage with influential figures such as Tony Robbins, NY Times Best Selling

Author and Speaker John Maxwell, Gary Keller, Piers Morgan, NY Times Best Selling Author Jon Gordon, NY Times Best Selling Author Malcolm Gladwell and Dr. Oz.

Tricia genuinely cares about empowering others. Her mission is to help you uncover and amplify your unique talents and strengths, turning them into unstoppable momentum. Whether you're ready to become a keynote speaker, craft a bestselling book, or coauthor with top-tier thought leaders, Tricia is dedicated to helping you leverage your expertise and elevate your brand.

How Tricia Can Help You:

1. **Speak on Stages:** Become a sought-after speaker who captivates audiences with a universally resonant message. Tricia will coach you on crafting your signature talk, refining your delivery, and securing speaking opportunities that amplify your voice and impact.

2. **Teach and Train:** Your knowledge and experience are meant to be shared. Learn to create proprietary products for passive income that you can sell repeatedly, extending your reach and influence.

3. **Write Your Book:** Whether it's your first book or your next bestselling project, Tricia will guide you through the writing process. She will help turn your expertise into a tangible product that establishes you as a leader in your field.

4. **Collaborate with Elite Leaders:** Imagine coauthoring a book with high caliber thought leaders. This collaboration can exponentially grow your reach and expose you to new audiences. Tricia offers rare opportunities to a select group of leaders to coauthor alongside her, enhancing their brand, exposure, credibility, and media opportunities.

5. **Provide You A Custom Roadmap:** Tricia has become an Authority in her field providing a high-level view of one's marketing strategy from brand story and messaging to offline presentation such as elevator pitch and in-person presentation to online presence such as online website with lead generation and elements that include how to develop a plan to present yourself on stages, podcasts, YouTube and other channels as well as how to create multiple streams of income such as courses, memberships, and polished keynotes and presentations that pulls all of your business vision all together with one coach and one solution. Imagine having a coach that understands everything you want to accomplish.

Tricia's work has been featured on platforms like Dr. Oz, Faith Unveiled Network, UplifTV, FOX, NBC, and CBS. Her creative and entrepreneurial legacy is a unique blend of practical business insights and artistic innovation. Tricia is also a singer and a fine artist, with her work displayed in galleries across the U.S.

Why wait? It's time to step onto the stage, write your book, and share your message with the world. Visit **www.TriciaAndreassen.com** to learn more her speaking, CreateCoreU.com to learn about her AI Marketing and Coaching University. Email Tricia at LiveLifeCreateYou@Gmail.com

Tricia and her sister Karen

TRANSFORMATIVE LEADERSHIP: CREATING RESILIENCE THROUGH KICKBUTT LEADERSHIP AND SERVANT LEADERSHIP

By Coni Meyers, LMC, CBLC, CDC

TRANSFORMATIVE LEADERSHIP: CREATING RESILIENCE THROUGH KICKBUTT LEADERSHIP AND SERVANT LEADERSHIP

A Journey of Empathy and Vision

In today's fast-paced world, leadership is evolving. Leaders are required to be visionaries, empathetic connectors, and conscious creators of opportunity for themselves and their teams. A few years ago, I wrote a certification course called Kickbutt Leadership, which has now become a term to describe a type of leadership where mindfulness meets vision, opportunity, and engagement, ultimately creating resiliency. It was important to show how to be an effective leader who empowers others and fosters qualities that shape truly transformative leaders.

At the heart of this dynamic lies' servant leadership, a philosophy introduced by Robert K. Greenleaf, perfectly aligning with the tenets of Kickbutt Leadership. It enhances its impact through empathy and dedication to others. The philosophy emphasizes that leaders should serve their teams first, prioritizing their needs and well-being above all else. This servant-first mentality fosters a culture of trust, empathy, and collaboration—qualities essential for resilience.

The Kickbutt philosophy provides a path to a clear vision, creating opportunities for engagement that make servant leadership so powerful. This focus on service builds trust, loyalty, and commitment, which, in turn, strengthens resilience. When individuals feel valued and supported by their leaders, they are more likely to go the extra mile, adapt to change, and persevere in the face of adversity.

Today, a leader's role is to provide a safe and nurturing environment where people feel encouraged to grow, take risks, and learn from failure. In doing so, they build resilience not just within themselves but throughout the entire organization. Embracing this approach, Kickbutt Leaders create a culture that views challenges as opportunities for collective growth, where team members are empowered to bounce back stronger than ever. As servant leaders, they engage their teams actively.

The Tapestry of Leading

Kickbutt Leadership represents a mindful approach to leading with impact, purpose, and respect for both the people you lead and the broader world in which you operate. It's a leadership style that harnesses the power of mindfulness to enhance emotional intelligence, foster a clear and compelling vision to drive collective action, and create an environment where people feel empowered to seize opportunities and engage with passion.

In this chapter, we explore how these concepts form a powerful leadership framework that transcends traditional models. We examine how mindfulness, vision, opportunity, and engagement are woven into the fabric of a Kickbutt leader's approach and how this, in turn, aligns with the philosophy of Servant Leadership. Servant leadership turns traditional leadership on its head. Instead of focusing on exerting power, servant leaders prioritize the needs and growth of their team members. They lead with empathy, humility, and a genuine desire to help others succeed.

My entire life has been centered around Kickbutt and Servant Leadership, even before I had a name for it. Early in my career, I was named rookie of the year for a major insurance company.

A year later, I became one of their first female sales managers and was given a team of four agents that was ranked 47th out of 48 teams in sales. In less than a year, our team was transformed.

At 27, with an accounting background, I had experience as a business manager but none in running a sales team. My team consisted of three older gentlemen, two from England and one from Italy. The woman on the team was trying to make ends meet on welfare. They saw me, this young woman, and doubted what I could do for them since they were older and experienced in insurance. Initially, the men wouldn't even sit down in my office. I quickly realized I needed to do something different than what they were used to. This company had just started offering car and homeowners insurance, but my team wanted to stay in their role as "debit agents" for life insurance.

From my accounting background, where planning and budgeting for the future were crucial, I decided we needed to create a vision for each agent. What did they want to achieve by year's end? Little did I know this was the beginning of the Kickbutt philosophy. They had never been asked about anything other than policy sales volumes.

When I asked each about their year's end goals, the three older men had the same answer: retirement. The woman wanted to be off welfare. As debit agents, they had an opportunity to talk about additional life insurance and, with the new property and casualty insurance, a chance to discuss their clients' car and home insurance needs.

At first, they were reluctant because they didn't know much about the new insurance type. I explained how property and casualty insurance offered ongoing commissions as long as clients stayed. This could increase their retirement funds and help the woman leave welfare. They simply needed to shift their mindset from offering only life insurance.

Once they realized the potential benefits, with a little education and support, they understood the value for their clients and themselves. With a clear vision for what they wanted and a perfect opportunity, they just needed the engagement component. I accompanied them on client meetings to help them get comfortable discussing new offerings. We converted over 60% of their clients to the new insurance options.

No longer hesitant to communicate, they now called me their "Manageress." By serving their wants and needs, they realized that serving clients not only benefited them but made clients more loyal. Each achieved their vision by year's end.

I also brought on four new agents who articulated what they wanted and were successful from the start. Our diverse team rose from 47th to second place in the Western region and fifth nationally.

What is Kickbutt Leadership?

Kickbutt Leadership isn't just a catchy phrase; it's a philosophy of leading with heart and purpose, mixed with a bit of grit. To kick butt means making things happen, having the courage to dream big, acting intentionally, and creating a lasting impact. It's also about leading with empathy, grace, and self-awareness. Kickbutt leaders understand that leadership isn't about dominating; it's about fostering collaboration, encouraging innovation, and serving the people who make the organization thrive, by being servant leaders. That's right. Serving from the heart is at the core. And to do this there are 4 Key Components that make everything flow in the way a Leader would envision it for long term success.

1. **Mindfulness** in leadership is about being fully present and aware, allowing leaders to operate with clarity and empathy. This heightened state of awareness allows leaders to operate with clarity and focus, enabling them to make empathetic and effective decisions. Mindful leaders can tune into the needs and concerns of their teams in real-time, improving communication and fostering an environment where team members feel heard and understood. This practice of mindfulness also cultivates self-awareness—a key trait for authentic and responsible leadership—by helping leaders understand their own emotional triggers, strengths, and weaknesses. As a result, mindful leaders can manage stress more effectively, avoid burnout, and support their teams through challenges with empathy and thoughtfulness.

Tips for Practicing Mindfulness

1. Daily Reflection: Set aside time each day to reflect on your thoughts and emotions, helping to build self-awareness.

2. Focus on Breathing: Use breathing exercises to stay calm and focused on stressful situations.

3. Active Listening: Practice truly listening to your team members, focusing on their words without interrupting.

2. **Vision** serves as the guiding star for Kickbutt Leadership, providing direction and inspiration for the future. A leader with a clear and compelling vision motivates team members to stretch beyond their current limitations and contribute to

a larger purpose. This vision not only aligns the team's efforts towards a common goal but also resonates with their hearts and minds, ensuring that each member understands the significance of their contributions. A powerful vision inspires action, ignites passion, and fosters a shared commitment to the organization's overarching mission. Moreover, leaders with a visionary outlook prioritize long-term goals and impact, striving to create positive change not only within the organization but also in the broader community.

Tips for Crafting a Vision

1. Communicate Clearly: Share your vision in a way that resonates with your team's values and aspirations.
2. Set Measurable Goals: Break down the vision into achievable goals that guide the team's efforts.
3. Inspire Passion: Regularly remind team members how their work contributes to the broader vision.

3. **Opportunity** is a crucial element of Kickbutt Leadership, as it involves actively seeking and creating pathways for growth, innovation, and success. Great leaders do not simply set a vision; they work diligently to unlock potential within their teams by identifying opportunities that foster professional and personal development. By providing tools, resources, and support, leaders empower their team members to take initiative, embrace challenges, and achieve their full potential. This focus on opportunity nurtures a culture of empowerment and engagement, where individuals feel motivated to contribute ideas and take ownership of their work. Additionally, leaders who champion innovation and risk-taking inspire their teams to think creatively and push the boundaries of what is possible.

Tips for Creating Opportunities

1. Encourage Innovation: Foster an environment where team members feel safe to explore new ideas.
2. Provide Resources: Offer training and development opportunities that align with team members' career goals.
3. Support Risk-Taking: Celebrate learning from failures as a step towards innovation and growth.

4. **Engagement** is essential for building trust and fostering connection within a team. It involves creating an inclusive and supportive environment where team members feel valued, respected, and connected to each other and the mission. Engaged leaders actively listen to their teams, provide constructive feedback, and show appreciation for their efforts, which helps to cultivate a sense of belonging and accountability. Empathy is at the heart of engagement, as leaders who understand and appreciate the experiences of their team members can address their needs effectively. This empathetic approach fosters psychological safety, encouraging team members to take risks, share ideas, and challenge the status quo without fear of judgment. As a result, engagement not only enhances morale but also leads to improved collaboration, problem-solving, and innovation.

Tips for Enhancing Engagement

1. Foster Inclusion: Ensure all team members have a voice and feel respected within the group.

2. Regular Feedback: Provide constructive feedback and recognition regularly to motivate and guide team members.

3. Empathy in Action: Show genuine care and support for your team's well-being, both professionally and personally.

The Holistic Approach

Kickbutt Leadership combines mindfulness, vision, opportunity, and engagement to create a dynamic and resilient leadership style. By being fully present, leaders can engage with their teams empathetically and with clarity. A compelling vision inspires and motivates, guiding teams toward shared goals with purpose and passion. By identifying and creating opportunities, leaders empower their teams to innovate and grow. Finally, fostering engagement builds trust and connection, ensuring that team members feel valued and empowered to contribute their best work. This holistic approach not only elevates leaders but also cultivates thriving, resilient teams capable of achieving extraordinary results.

Servant Leadership Reflections

1. How can you integrate mindfulness into your daily leadership practices to enhance your presence and clarity?

_____

_____

_____

_____

_____

2. What strategies can you use to communicate your vision effectively and inspire your team?

_____
_____
_____
_____
_____
_____

3. In what ways can you create opportunities for your team members to grow and innovate?

_____
_____
_____
_____
_____
_____

4. How can you foster a culture of engagement that values and includes every team member's contribution?

_____
_____
_____
_____
_____
_____

5. What actions can you take to demonstrate empathy and understanding towards your team's needs and experiences?

_____
_____
_____
_____
_____
_____
_____

AUTHOR BIOGRAPHY

Here is a free workbook on becoming a Kickbutt and Servant Leader: **https://linktr.ee/kickbutt**

Coni Meyers, LMC, CBLC, CDC

Coni Meyers is a force of nature. Her extensive experience and expertise in crisis management and leadership have made her a renowned figure in the field. Coni is a 7X international bestselling author and speaker. She is dedicated to ensuring that individuals and communities become sustainable and are well-prepared during times of disaster.

Through CKMP, Coni has tirelessly worked to educate and support thousands of individuals and businesses in their sustainability and crisis preparedness efforts. Her decades of dedication have left a lasting impact on those she has worked with, equipping them with the knowledge and tools to navigate and manage their efforts effectively.

Coni's commitment extends beyond her work with CKMP. As a FEMA inspector, she has played a crucial role in educating and training communities and their citizens on the importance of preparedness and crisis management. Her efforts have helped to strengthen resilience and empower individuals to face and overcome challenges.

Coni's impact on the business world is also notable. Two companies she co-founded, WIN Home Inspections and OnlineEd, she helped transform into national enterprises.

Recognizing the need for effective leadership in all spheres of life, she founded CKM Solutions Group, Crystalline Moments Success Movement, and Kickbutt Leadership. These entities focus on inspiring and empowering individuals to reach their full potential.

Coni's vibrant personality is evident in her work and interactions. Full of energy, passion, and grit, she approaches every endeavor with enthusiasm and determination. Her contagious spirit ignites motivation and fosters a sense of purpose in everyone she encounters.

Through her multifaceted contributions and unwavering dedication. Coni Meyers has emerged as a true visionary and leader in sustainability, crisis management, and leadership. Her remarkable achievements and commitment to helping others make her an inspirational figure in the field.

Founder & President
CKM Preparedness Foundation
Kits4Kids-Info
https://www.BePreparedBeReady.org

PRACTICING SERVANT LEADERSHIP ARTISAN

By Alvaro "Al" Ferreira

PRACTICING SERVANT LEADERSHIP ARTISAN

(What do I want folks to walk away with: Why I chose Servant Leadership and my mistakes of trying to be a hierarchical leader.)

Reflecting on Servant Leadership: My Journey
In my 45 summers of experience, I've realized the remarkable efficacy of **Servant Leadership** in running organizations. As someone who has spent most of my career as a youth development professional, specifically in managing summer camps and outdoor environmental education, I've come to appreciate how this leadership style is uniquely suited to our environment. **Servant Leadership** is all about focusing on the growth and well-being of our staff and the people we serve, namely our campers and their families.

The beauty of this approach lies in its core focus on the needs of others. When people feel valued and well-supported, they find themselves in an inclusive space where they can flourish. This atmosphere, where individuals can grow and thrive, is what sets **Servant Leadership** apart. I've found that by empowering my staff and stepping aside, they take on a sense of ownership and accountability that's truly transformative. Our collective efforts have led to countless meaningful and life-changing experiences for our campers.

At the heart of **Servant Leadership** is trust and collaboration. In any organization, serving others and nurturing a culture of well-being is paramount. Through my years, I've identified five essential priorities that underscore the efficacy of **Servant Leadership**:

1. Being camper-centered, or customer-centered, creates a culture that values and supports individuals, fostering an inclusive environment where growth and thriving are encouraged.

2. By empowering staff with a focus on their well-being, we see greater ownership and heightened accountability. Empowered staff members are more likely to create meaningful and impactful experiences for campers.

3. Cultivating a culture of trust is vital for teamwork. When staff feels heard and respected, collaboration improves, and feedback becomes open and constructive, which enhances operations at all levels.

4. Many of our staff are in their first job, and we have a duty to nurture their personal and professional growth. The skills they develop are crucial for their futures, impacting both their leadership abilities and our campers.

5. Positive energy and strong relationships are essential for camps, as they are in any great workplace. Servant Leadership exemplifies and encourages humility, empathy, and care—qualities that foster a warm, supportive, and fun atmosphere.

Servant Leadership aligns seamlessly with values commonly found in summer camps: community, personal growth, and meaningful impact, making it an ideal leadership style for such settings.

I've experienced both incredible successes and challenging moments as a leader. Often, these outcomes have stemmed from choices I've made. Much like the opening of Dickens' novel, I can reflect on my journey by saying, "I am born." I remember the day I began to embrace the principles of Servant Leadership, and how it has shaped my path ever since.

Incredibly, the principles outlined here are now clearly interwoven throughout this book, as I share my experiences and the leadership styles that have emerged throughout my career.

Servant Leader: My Beginnings

I first encountered the term "Servant Leader" in late fall of 1986, thanks to Wally Wirick, one of my first mentors at the YMCA Camp Bluff Lake. Wally and Sam Brown, who ran the downtown YMCA in Pasadena, had just attended a retreat in San Diego with Rich Collato, where they learned how to support their staff for collective success.

"I've learned that people will forget what you said, people will forget what you did, but people will never forget how you made them feel." - Maya Angelou's

Reflecting on my life, I can trace much of it back to a few key events and individuals. I resonate deeply with These early leaders set the bar for how to make people feel, and I'm recounting moments from over 40 years ago that they inspired.

Before we ran a camp session in 1983, a pivotal meeting at the downtown YMCA in Pasadena with Ron Perry started it all. Alongside another team member from Temple City Y, I embarked on this journey at the urging of our program director, Maxine. We sought guidance on hosting a YMCA camp at Bluff Lake, and

Ron provided a gracious and clear overview. It was a formal business meeting, the first of many to follow. During that summer of '83, I began to discover who I was meant to be.

One defining moment occurred during a break with my junior leader, Mike Nordin. While taking shelter from the rain in the KYBO—the camp's restroom and shower facility—Ron, the camp director, stopped by. A large, engaging figure, Ron had a presence everyone was drawn to. After checking in with us, he surprisingly offered us 20 extra minutes of break, pulling two bottles of soda from his back pockets and volunteering to cover our cabin. As Ron walked out, I turned to Mike and said, "someday I want his job."

At the time, I couldn't fully grasp what that entailed. Ron exemplified true leadership. Through his service, I learned the importance of leading by serving others—a theme encapsulated by John Maxwell's Law of Legacy: "Leadership is the one thing you cannot delegate." This moment in time was a thoughtful exercise.

"Leadership is simply about influencing people. Nothing more, nothing less." – John Maxwell's 2nd Law of Influence.

MAC vs PC - Lessons in Servant Leadership

I Am Your Biggest Fan

That journey of Servant Leadership and the subsequent displays of traditional hierarchical leadership have equipped me to know that the better model is PC over Mac. Despite the title of this section, I am not here to extol the virtues of any particular computer. In fact, I am here to share about two vastly different leadership styles.

Let me share a bit about Mac. He came to camp to help lead our leaders in training programs (LITs). He had excellent interviews, and he talked a great deal about service. Mac's references praised his work with teens. Mac said he was looking for a new opportunity to learn and grow as part of a team.

At this point in my career, I had learned to invest in leadership. When I hired someone as part of our team, I was their biggest fan. Early in my life as a YMCA Camp Director, an old Y guy, Dan, told me this "idea" about hiring people. He said, "Make sure you hire someone that you know you are going to fire during that training week. That way you make a point with the rest of the staff, and they will do what you want." I thought this was great. I was included in the secrets of being a director.

Dan, whom I admired, shared what I thought was a secret that would make me a better director—not necessarily a leader. So, I did this. During that week, I knew that Gus was the person. He had a tough time with direction, yet he was likable. When the time came, I made it public, thinking I orchestrated it well. I told Gus, "You're done. Your services here are no longer needed." I won't describe what happened next; it was not pretty, nor am I proud of any of it.

I felt like a "BOSS" that day. I thought my staff would listen to everything, and for a brief time they did. But later, I felt sick to my stomach—a pattern that repeated in similar situations.

I would love to say I changed that practice immediately. I believed it was necessary to stomach through it because Dan wouldn't suggest it otherwise. For several years, I did just that. To Gus, Debbie, Mike, Pete, Simon, and Shirley, I apologize. It took time to realize that leading a team from a place of fear was not where I wanted to be as a leader.

For the past 31 years or so, I've hired each person expecting the best. I have been their biggest fan. John Maxwell teaches a simple thought: "Put a 10 on their heads." This is what I did with Mac.

Different Approaches

PC had been at the camp for a while, serving as our operations leader and essentially our "second in command." PC sought out multiple certifications in different areas of camp. Someone once referred to PC as an overachiever.

Mac wanted to be creative and try different things with the program. PC focused on creating order in what many camp folks know as chaos.

The Incident

In the fifth week of camp, roles were well-defined, and early challenges were past. One night, PC was working late in the office, downloading and preparing session rosters, activity lists, and check-in forms. PC was meticulous, always working ahead to ensure smooth operations.

Mac was also in the office, planning for the end of the next LIT session. Mac had made significant progress with the LITs, who adored him and were drawn to his style. He regularly engaged other staff on LIT management, often dictating expectations for each LIT during activities.

James, a unit leader, seeking advice from our assistant program director, Jeff, was interrupted by Mac. The conversation quickly derailed as Mac told James to "man up" or risk losing control. Mac insisted his LITs followed his rules faithfully, and others should follow suit.

PC overheard the escalating situation. With a commanding presence, PC excused everyone except Mac from the room. Jeff, alarmed, called me, and I arrived to meet James and Jeff outside the office. Inside, I could hear Mac's heated voice. PC, recognizing the need for resolution, had stepped in where needed most.

The Gazelle

Before I move along in the story, let me share a bit about the Gazelle. I have long been fascinated by any organization or culture that broadcasts permission giving as part of their environment. I had an anthropology class in college, and I remember the professor saying, "people don't paint their toenails, cultures do." That statement always made me think about what we allow and what we tolerate.

One non-profit that I worked with had an annual retreat for middle and senior staff. This was usually an away event, and everyone was asked to ride a tour bus to and from and spend the two nights together. One of the afternoon/evenings always involved some sort of competition of artificially devised teams. This was a particularly extreme hierarchical structured organization.

The evening always had some drinking of adult beverages and the senior most staff would talk about the Gazelles. This "tradition" was explained to me (somewhat proudly) to determine who fit into the culture and who would be the gazelle at the outskirt of the herd. When that gazelle (staff member) took too much of a risk or perhaps did not control themselves due to drinking and a permissive culture, the lions would pounce. It was particularly cruel, and I was grateful that I had a long-standing rule never to drink anything that would inhibit my behavior at a work event.

I walked into the office. PC was sitting in a chair, hands clasped in what appeared to be a listening stance that I had grown to expect from him. Mac was pacing and talking about how people at that camp needed to manage their staff if he would do it himself. I sat on the desk with my back up against the wall and asked, "I'd like to know what has been going on. Mac, let's start with you."

Within 15 minutes, we had reached a state of truce and agreements as to how we would proceed and behave. I can't claim credit for that since PC had already initiated most of what needed to occur. He wanted there to be growth because of the experience and I concurred.

It was a form of dedication that PC really exemplified. I looked this word up in the dictionary and surprisingly it did not have PC's picture next to it. It does say, "to set apart seriously for a special purpose." If there were a mark in anyone's lifetime, this would be PC. He always talked about the campers and what he did to help them so that they could have an enjoyable time at Camp. This was PC's special purpose, and he took it seriously.

The rest of that summer became about the leadership cult of Mac versus the value of service from and as exemplified by PC. Lessons learned.

"Leadership is learned over time. Leaders are always learners."- John Maxwell, 3rd Law of Leadership reminds us that it is always about the process.

Here is what I have learned. Simply put, culture is how we work together every day. I have become, over these four and a half decades, a Servant Leader. A practicing Servant Leader artisan.

Practice comes from doing things that work and learning from the things that don't work. It is the habits I have developed and modeled for others. I know that architects, doctors, and lawyers have a practice, and I believe that any time you are a leader you are in practice of those skills and abilities as well.

The artisan is someone who makes things either in a traditional or non-mechanized way using high-quality ingredients, like local artisan cheese. Leadership is an art and a skill, and one can develop those skills and continue to get better throughout their career.

The traditional model of Servant Leadership points to Jesus Christ. Whether you are a believer, non-believer, or a historian, He modeled the way and was the original Servant Leader.

"For even the Son of Man came not to be served but to serve, and to give his life as a ransom for many." - Mark 10:45

In a recent survey, the Arbinger Institute - revealed that 100% of workplace challenges were reported to "tie back to people and culture issues, yet only 27% agree that their company's culture impacts their ability to meet or exceed goals."

There are some basic ways to determine your leadership style and begin to move further towards Servant Leadership. I've learned that putting others ahead of myself is a needed amount of self-sacrifice. It is that deliberate attempt to foster collaboration and inclusivity. As an individual nurtures others, it is a key aspect of Servant Leadership.

Servant Leadership Reflections

1. When working in a team, how do you ensure that everyone's voice is heard? Are you a Mac or a PC?

   _____
   _____
   _____
   _____
   _____
   _____
   _____
   _____
   _____

2. How do you handle situations where someone is overlooked or is on the fringe of the team?

   _____
   _____
   _____
   _____
   _____
   _____
   _____
   _____
   _____

3. What steps do you take to empower and support them when they are working and struggling to achieve their goals?

_____
_____
_____
_____
_____
_____
_____
_____
_____

4. How do you prioritize the needs of others over your own (even when it is inconvenient or challenging)?

_____
_____
_____
_____
_____
_____
_____
_____
_____
_____
_____

AUTHOR BIOGRAPHY
Alvaro "Al" Ferreira

Born in Natal, Brazil, I immigrated to the United States with my family at the age of four. Growing up in Pasadena, California, I attended California State Polytechnic University, Pomona, earning a degree in Communications with a focus on Journalism and Organizational Communication.

My journey as a youth development professional began at the age of 15 when I joined the YMCA. Over the course of more than four decades, I've served in various non-profit leadership roles, directing and leading multiple YMCA and Scout camps. My efforts have positively impacted over 54,000 campers, creating meaningful experiences that foster growth and leadership.

For 43 summers, I have embraced the role of a servant leader, dedicated to empowering young leaders in outdoor educational and residential camp settings. My work has included recruiting, training, and mentoring thousands of teens and young adults to realize their leadership potential. My passion for leadership development has driven me to create progressive programs and facilitate organizational development experiences for youth, teens, college students, volunteer boards, and staff. My mission has always been clear: to provide lessons that inspire "Leaders for Life."

As a certified coach, speaker, and trainer through the John C. Maxwell Team, I've further honed my ability to mentor and develop future leaders. I've had the privilege of redesigning the Easton Foundation's Olympic Archery in Schools curriculum, now offered at over 170 schools and three major Foundation locations across the United States.

In addition to my work in youth development, I've co-hosted the *Youth Development Leadership* podcast with Michael Garcia and regularly contribute to my blog, *Leadership from Al Ferreira Coaching*, where I share insights and strategies for empowering others.

Among my proudest moments are the days my children—Alec, Kelly Rose, and Brian—were born, the day I married my wife, Lee Anne, and the day I became an American citizen.

"It is my passion to support those who lead and serve others."

I am a passionate advocate for character development, dedicated to helping organizations unlock their full potential through meaningful growth. With a deep understanding of personal values and practical skills, I have designed and delivered impactful curricula that inspire character values like resilience, empathy, and leadership.

My innovative approach combines time tested strategies with engaging activities, empowering participants to build confidence, strengthen relationships, and navigate life's challenges with integrity.

Consider my approach in collaborating to develop transformative experiences that nurtures lasting character and meaningful success.

I am at alfatcamp@gmail.com, LinkedIn (https://www.linkedin.com/in/alferreira42/), and 585.969.3162

BECOMING A SERVANT LEADER: MY JOURNEY

By Wendy Gunn

IS BECOMING A SERVANT LEADER: MY JOURNEY

Have you ever wanted to be a leader? A servant leader? Have you wanted to take on the role of leader but ditch the servant part? Yeah, me too. This is my story of how God transformed me into an unlikely servant leader—someone He can use in the lives of others.

I haven't always been the "confident, successful," goal-achieving Christian woman, entrepreneur, and coach I am today. There was a time I found myself trapped in a cycle of comparing myself to others, trying to mimic my friends by taking pieces from their lives to patch up mine. I felt inferior and miserable. Severely obese, I carried not only extra physical weight but also the heavy burden of feeling "not enough."

God never intended for me to live this way. He wanted to remind me that even if you could succeed in copying someone else's life, you would miss God's unique purpose for creating you. The Bible reminds us that we were "wonderfully and marvelously woven in our mother's womb," a truth I had overlooked while entangled in the lives of others.

Discovering True Leadership

Leadership, as John Maxwell succinctly puts it, does not require natural talent, but demands a heart devoted to God and a willingness to learn. Leadership is often defined as "the ability of an individual or a group to influence and guide followers or members of an organization, society, or team." But what about servant leadership? A servant leader serves first and leads by example. Jesus was the perfect servant leader, guiding His followers with compassion and humility. True leadership manifests when others are positively influenced by your actions and words—when you've experienced the impact of a truly great leader, you recognize their significance instantly.

The Call to Servant Leadership

Is everyone called to be a servant leader? As followers of Jesus, the answer is yes.

With the Holy Spirit's power, we are to use our God-given gifts to make a difference in the lives of others. Leadership in this context refers to "stewarding one's gifts, abilities, and opportunities to influence and serve others." Imagine a world where every believer obeys the command to make disciples with this servant's heart.

Servant leaders remain grounded in the teachings of Jesus, striving daily to serve others through actions empowered by the Holy Spirit. Our efforts, when led by Him, result in spiritually fruitful living. We lead others by following Jesus closely, powered by the love and strength He provides, creating a path for others to follow.

The Superhero Paradox

The world loves superheroes. Perhaps this fascination stems from God, the ultimate Superhero. With His Spirit dwelling in us, we are transformed into superheroes of service, but all the glory belongs to Him.

To become the servant leader God calls me to be, I first had to lead myself. This transformation does not occur without trials.

God guides His servants into leadership through challenges, expanding their horizons beyond the small worlds they knew when entrapped by comparison and competition.

Becoming a servant leader is an ongoing journey that begins with leading oneself. To steward one's God-given gifts, abilities, and opportunities effectively requires introspection and personal transformation, often through life's trials. This is a story of such a transformation.

God shapes His servants into leaders through trials. I had been living small, ensnared in comparison, mimicry, competition, and envy. Yet, God had bigger plans for me, which began to unfold during an unexpected life event.

Leading with Purpose through Adversity

Our family had the pleasure of hosting two young Japanese women, owing to our connection to family missionaries in Japan. My son, 15, and daughter, 12, were thrilled to introduce our guests to American culture and fun activities, which included a trip to the Mall of America. This was a familiar ritual to help our guests adjust to jet lag.

As we entered the Mall, I was struck by an intense abdominal pain, fearing its source as unknown, yet just short of catastrophic like appendicitis. I left the guests in the adept hands of my children, seeking refuge in the nearest restroom, hoping for relief.

The pain, however, was relentless, leaving me no choice but to attempt the drive home, pressing my fist against my abdomen to stave off the waves of agony. Once home, a night's sleep miraculously erased the pain.

The subsequent days mirrored a flu-like state, accompanied by a fever and an overall sense of malaise, but I persisted for the sake of our planned activities. After the guests departed, a concerning lapse in normalcy prompted me to contact a nurse.

Her directive was clear and urgent: see my doctor that day or visit Urgent Care. A sense of divine timing echoed through her compassionate instructions. My faith saw me through, believing that God was paving the path for something beyond my understanding.

My physician, a fellow Christian, was instrumental that day. His decision to not dismiss my symptoms but rather to investigate through a CT scan was nothing short of providential. This scan, followed by my husband's unusual presence at the appointment, revealed a startling truth: tumors, not cysts, had taken hold and spread.

Thus began my battle with ovarian cancer—a journey not anticipated nor desired, yet one that redefined my life's purpose. Each step of the way, servant leaders emerged, guiding and supporting us. This experience crystallized my understanding of servant leadership: a call not just to serve but to lead others through the service, inspired and directed by divine purpose. This trial was the crucible in which God reshaped me. It was more than just a battle for life; it was a battle for purpose and identity, one that I am now grateful for. Through it all, I emerged with a mission to share with others the truth that each of us is uniquely created for a purpose. I believe wholeheartedly that discovering and living this purpose is a form of honoring our creation.

As I share this experience of growing in servant leadership, my story is not just about me; it extends an invitation to you to discover your unique purpose and to influence and serve those around you. Whether through life's unexpected challenges or its quiet moments of reflection, we are all called to be more than what we appear, to be servant leaders in God's hands.

The Silent Battle: A Journey of Resilience and Faith

Ovarian cancer is often referred to as the silent killer because its symptoms are subtle and easily overlooked until it becomes too late to address effectively. At the time of my diagnosis, the grim reality was that 85% of those diagnosed succumbed to the disease. This statistic hung over me like a dark cloud as I navigated the early days of my cancer journey.

After returning to our quiet home, nestled with our sleeping children, a profound realization struck me: the power of prayer was about to become a central element in my life. That night, before prayer chains were activated by my husband—a poignant role reversal that was the first of many—we had no network of prayer support yet. It was during these solitary hours that I truly learned the profound power of prayer. Without it, sleep eluded me as fears and worst-case scenarios filled my mind.

In the days that followed, I came to understand that servant leadership encompasses providing prayer support. It's not the least we can do; it is, in fact, the most powerful form of support we can offer. The exceptional peace, the almost tangible feeling of being lifted and supported by others' prayers, ignited in me a passion for seeking prayer without hesitation whenever a crisis arises.

We arrived at the clinic before it even opened, engulfed by a surreal sense of unreality as we analyzed the images from the scans. There was one apparent mass, but just one. If there were more, my untrained eyes couldn't detect them. For years, I wondered if there might be two. Confirmation came only a couple of years ago when I saw a copy of the written diagnosis. I had been right all along; there were indeed two football-sized tumors, both enormous and of similar size. Seeing it in black and white reassured me that it hadn't just been a figment of my imagination.

On that beautiful Wednesday morning in May, Dr. Hagstrom made a pivotal call, then turned to us with a question that would alter the course of my life. "If you could have surgery on Friday, (which was just two days later) would you want that?" he asked.

Our answer was immediate and unequivocal, "Yes."

God's work was manifesting at an incredible pace. I underwent surgery performed by one of the leading surgeons in the United States. Being in a teaching hospital at the University of Minnesota, a pioneer in various medical fields, meant that a dozen students often accompanied my doctor during visits.

On that Friday, Dr. Patricia Judson operated, discovering only one but still football-sized tumor. Remarkably, it was contained and could be removed. My cancer was caught early. That summer, I underwent chemotherapy, and I agreed to be part of a study examining the effects of weekly low-dose chemo treatments on the recurrence rate in rare cases like mine.

Discovering the Heart of Servant Leadership

Have you ever met someone who embodies the spirit of a servant leader? Their presence might not overwhelm you at first glance. Yet, through their quiet character, integrity, and their undeniable ability to "walk the talk," they impact you deeply. These leaders guide and influence through their essence—through who they are and Whose they are rather than their words or actions alone.

The distinction between a mere leader and a servant leader often rests upon their relationship with a higher authority, specifically with the Sovereign Creator, God Almighty, and their belief in His Son, Jesus Christ. This submission to divine authority is foundational. Before leading others, a servant leader first submits themselves to the sovereignty of God, acknowledging His grace and power through the sacrifice of His Son—a humbling yet empowering start to their leadership journey.

In aspiring to be a true servant leader, the first person you must lead is yourself. An insightful quote from William Penn states, "No man is fit to command another that cannot command himself," underscoring the necessity of self-leadership. This form of personal discipline is not always readily embraced but is crucial for effective leadership.

In my own life, God used a personal battle with cancer to grow both my desire and capacity to lead myself. In the year following my diagnosis, I embarked on a journey to healthier living, shedding 50 pounds in the process—one domino that triggered the fall of many others towards my transformation. Through this, God instilled in me a profound sense of discipline.

Discipline, though sometimes dreaded like the word "cancer," is indispensable in the realm of servant leadership. Jim Rohn eloquently put it, "Discipline is the bridge between goals and accomplishment." When I realized I could lose those fifty pounds through God's strength, it became evident that He could transform any area of my life. Reflecting on the words of Paul from 1 Corinthians 9:27, I was reminded of the importance of subjection and leading by example.

Many potential servant leaders stumble because they lack self-discipline, failing to lead their own lives and yielding to moral failures that stunt their potential. As Plato wisely observed, "The first and best victory is to conquer self." This journey of self-mastery is ongoing, as Paul alluded when he said, "Not that I have apprehended." We are constantly striving toward mastery, especially while we navigate this earthly journey.

Taking care of one's body is also critical to leadership. It is the "temple of the Holy Spirit," and thus must be respected and maintained. The impression we give is largely influenced by our physical presence and energy. Yet, God was far from finished with me even after my weight loss. As more dominoes fell, I became more organized, witnessed my children grow into adults who walked in faith, completed homeschooling from start to finish, and celebrated a nearly 50-year marriage.

Trials and experiences mold our character, deepen our discipline, reshape our mindsets, and extend our reach, allowing God to craft an incredible story through us. For the servant leader, achieving God's goals is intertwined with their leadership. They lead by setting and reaching these goals, showing others the way by blazing trails grounded in faith and perseverance.

By God's Grace: A Journey of Transformation and Servant Leadership

After the age of 60, I defied the odds and lost another 50 pounds, bringing my total weight loss to nearly 100 pounds.

This journey of personal transformation empowered me to take my entire family on a dream trip to Italy, all thanks to the miles I'd diligently saved up. Alongside this, I launched my online business and watched my email list blossom to 12,000 subscribers in just over 24 months, boasting an impressive 37% open rate.

Every step I took was a testament to the principle that God's ways often stand in contrast to the ways of the world. He has crafted each of us uniquely, not to blend in, but to rise above, distinguished by unique stories that reflect His steadfast faithfulness through our struggles and His power in our triumphs. It's our responsibility to shine brightly, glorifying Him through our lives.

Embracing servant leadership, we are all called to make disciples and lead by serving others. Faithfulness to God reigns as the supreme character trait essential for any servant leader. It's a quality that runs through the veins of true leadership.

In this world, a faithful Christian's life may seem unremarkable. We may never taste fame or perform deeds that captivate worldly eyes. However, by stewarding our God-given talents, abilities, and opportunities, and by using them to influence and serve others, we exhibit the kind of faithfulness that begins with the little things. As Luke 16:10 (KJV) states, "He that is faithful in that which is least is faithful also in much: and he that is unjust in the least is unjust also in much."

The eyes of many watch us, and our ultimate aim should be to hear those precious words from God: "Well done, good and faithful servant."

Has God transformed my life through trials and unlocked doors of servant leadership through the lessons He has imparted? Yes, that's how He works. The way we respond to trials can either embitter us or better us. These trials serve as pathways to greater servant leadership and help reinforce the character traits we may lack. They provide an opportunity to display Christlike character to a world watching to see if God is real and Christianity is true.

For six months, I encountered the same doctors and nurses weekly during clinical study, plus the initial three months of chemo treatments every three weeks. This formed a nine-month bond with the cancer center nurses and doctors. I became a bold advocate, sharing God's work in my life with them, and they were an attentive audience.

Despite their admirable service and our mutual affection, I wouldn't classify the cancer center nurses as servant leaders. Their care was tireless and sacrificial, ministering profoundly to my body and soul. Strong, capable, decisive, intelligent, kind, caring, and hard-working, they excelled in their profession. Yet, to my knowledge, they did not believe in Jesus Christ.

Reflecting on my cancer experience and diving deep into the meaning of servant leadership has reinforced my belief that faith in and following Jesus Christ is essential for true servant leadership.

Embracing Servant Leadership Through Submission

At the heart of servant leadership is a profound submission to the authority of the Creator, who designed us with purpose. As a servant leader, the journey begins with following, serving, and obeying our King, Jesus. This path of service is an extension of His commandment to love Him fully—with all our hearts, souls, minds, and strength—and to love others as ourselves.

God often places us in situations where our weaknesses become a canvas for His strength and power. It is a humbling process, encapsulated by the mindset that He must increase, and we must decrease. Are we willing to become less, allowing His light to shine brightly through us? This journey requires earnest dedication, a readiness to follow closely after Him, and a daily commitment to say, "I'm available. Here am I. Send me."

The call to follow Him is a call to surrender, whatever the circumstances. It's about learning to wait on Him, trusting that He is the 'how' in every situation. He may not reveal what lies ahead, but He assures us of His presence at every moment, exercising control over it all.

God desires for our lives to be a testament to His power at work in us. Through trials, He transforms us, shaping us into servant leaders if we are open to His guidance. By embodying faithfulness, both in example and character, our lives can exemplify servant leadership. Those who observe us and follow our path may also become servant leaders, as they see us pointing consistently to Jesus. Ultimately, through this journey, God is always glorified.

Servant Leadership Reflections

1. How has comparing yourself to others impacted your personal growth? How could you change this going forward after hearing my story?

___

2. In what ways can you lead by serving others right now?

___

3. Can you think of a time when a leader influenced you resulting in a positive impact on your life?

4. What gifts or abilities can you use to serve others most effectively?

5. Reflect on a trial in your life and how it shaped your leadership abilities for serving yourself and others?

AUTHOR BIOGRAPHY
Wendy Gunn

Wendy Gunn is a Christian entrepreneur and ovarian cancer survivor. She stopped comparing, copying, competing, and coveting her friends' lives when she was diagnosed with two football-sized tumors and realized her life and story were forever changed. Three days later, only one, still football-sized tumor was removed, and she knew she was uniquely created by God–a walking miracle and alive–for a purpose.

Integrating her faith in Christ with her personal and professional goal achievement, she is an example that God has a message to proclaim through you to the world, and He uses your trials to tell a story of His faithfulness to a watching world wanting to know if God is real and Christianity is true.

She helps clients achieve their big goals, no matter their age, including growing a thriving email list and losing weight, while boldly living out their faith in Christ.

Wendy's first book (on the topic of The Best Way to Build An Email List Fast) will be published in early 2025. She will be a speaker at the Global Women's Empowerment Summit in 2025. You can watch Wendy daily on her YouTube Channel, Your Home for God, and find her guesting on podcasts across your favorite podcast platforms.

Wendy has a gift for Christian entrepreneurs who desire to embrace who God uniquely created them to be and fulfill their purpose as servant leaders, "10 Questions to Identify Your Ideal Client Fast": https://yourhomeforgod.com/10-questions

Social Media Links:

Wendy Gunn can be found here:

Facebook:
https://facebook.com/wendygunnyourhomeforgod

Instagram:
https://instagram.com/wendygunnyourhomeforgod

LinkedIn:
https://linkedin.com/in/wendygunn/

YouTube Channel:
https://www.youtube.com/channel/UCmMr5g_UMZ1BStDYkJPEUyg

Website:
https://yourhomeforgod.com

Email:
wendygunn@yourhomeforgod.com

YOU ARE CREATED FOR GREATNESS

By Natalie Martin

YOU ARE CREATED FOR GREATNESS

It is both a great honor and privilege that I am preparing this chapter for the Co-Author Servant Leadership Book with Artist and #1 Best Selling Author, the Unstoppable Warrior, Tricia Andreassen. I've had the unique ability to connect personally with Tricia, she's a friend and great source of encouragement and leadership in my first co-author experience. She's taught me so much in our brief time together, she's an incredible inspiration and source of hope in a dark and gloomy world. When someone has a story as dark and incredibly painful as mine has been, it's a breath of fresh air to find someone, like Tricia, who took the time to invest time into helping me see the worth of my story and the value of my voice.

I've always said, even since childhood, that one day I would write a book. I thought my first publishing would be an autobiography because of the childhood and experiences life has presented to me would certainly make for an interesting read. Yet here I am writing my first work for publishing and while it's not an autobiography it's certainly a huge part of who I am, who I've always been and who I'm learning to accept and embrace as I've gained wisdom and encouragement from people like Tricia.

The topic, I'm sure you're aware of now, is Servant Leadership. It so happens that Servant Leadership is the epitome of my entire existence. I can't wait to share my perspective of Servant Leadership with you. I graciously thank you for spending time with me and the other authors of this book who have poured out their servant's heart into the chapters of this book. It's our desire, if I may so boldly speak for the group collectively, to share the true beauty of Servant Leadership with others to inspire and ignite a movement in leadership style that makes the world a better place to work and live.

You may be saying to yourself, who is this debut author that's so certain of her understanding for Servant Leadership? Well, I never thought you'd ask. I'm one of those "Raised on Dolly Parton and Sweet Tea" and "Runs on Coffee and Jesus" type of girls from the foothills of NC. I am proud of my Southern Heritage and the values, manners, kindness and the genuine hospitality my roots have instilled within me. I'm well educated with a MACC as my highest level of education, and I have many years of experience under my belt in both the Private Sector and in Public Education. I'm a God-girl, smitten wife and a loving mother to two precious children, a bonus son and an angel baby. I dare say I'm quite unique in personality, empathy, authenticity, loyalty and passionate about life and serving others. I'm yours truly, a debut author, Natalie Powell Martin. I'm blessed to be here working with these incredible authors!

When I was asked to be a Co-Author for this book, I was honored that I had made enough impression upon Tricia that she would even ask me. I was "just" a middle school business teacher at the time; what could I possibly know about Servant Leadership and writing a chapter in a book that would be published? Since her initial request I began praying and looking for ways to validate my ability to participate in this book. The Lord has revealed so much to me about myself and unveiled the perfectly orchestrated steps of my life that led me to this very moment.

Why Servant Leadership?

Servant Leadership is the highest level of leadership and management style an individual could strive for. Leading through service is selfless and sacrificial. When we choose to lead by example and to lead others by serving them; we release the need for power and control, we let go of our ego and we serve joyfully without hesitation. Servant Leadership isn't for the faint of heart and is quite challenging and demanding for those who choose this style of leadership; or might I suggest, this style of leadership chooses them.

Servant Leadership chose me, I wouldn't say that I was aware of this calling upon my life having a title or divine purpose. I knew that I was different and widely set apart, I am a giver when the world around me is filled with takers, I'm a doer constantly serving others while others tend to desire to be served. When I realized that 'who I was' had a title or label I was flabbergasted. For the first time in my life, I realized that God had called me to this. I went about my life as if it was just expected of me and part of who I was to do the things I did the way I did them. It didn't occur to me that I was set apart for a reason. All these years I viewed my characteristics as flaws but didn't seem to have the power within to change them. The realization of this "calling" brought tears to my eyes and finally the hardships of life and the sacrifices I've willingly endured made complete and total sense to me for the first time ever.

It Matters!

God calls us where He wants us and needs us for His purpose and plan. The rewards of Servant Leadership are far greater than the sacrifices one must make to fulfill this calling. I dare say that this form of leadership is more rewarding than any other form of leadership. It's a personal internal reward not one that must be announced or recognized. To know that you've impacted the life of one of God's children reminds us that we're doing something right, no matter how difficult the calling may be, it matters. It matters to the Servant Leader who sees the product of their work and realizes they are impacting the world around them one act of service at a time while carrying out the calling on their life. It matters to the Lord who has called us to be Servant Leaders that we're obedient and heed His calling, laying down our needs and desires to serve the needs and desires of our brothers and sisters in Christ. There's something special about being about the father's work!

The Bible tells us in John 7:18: "Whoever speaks on their own does so to gain personal glory, but he who seeks the glory of the one who sent him is a man of truth; there is nothing false about him." Therefore, we are called by Christ to seek the glory of God. When we seek our own glory, look for our horn to be tooted, desire all the accolades, awards, titles, compensation and recognition from others we take the beauty of Servant Leadership away. I'd say that Servant Leadership then shifts and becomes another form of leadership when we don't have a servant's heart. We must not seek earthly rewards, for our reward in heaven will be all the greater. Matthew 6:19-21: "Do not store up for yourselves treasures on earth, where moths and vermin destroy, and where thieves break in and steal. But store up for yourselves treasures in heaven, where moths and vermin do not destroy, and where thieves do not break in and steal. For where your treasure is, there your heart will be also." Servant Leaders who truly seek to serve the Lord do not look for recognition and applause. They look for ways to serve others without notice or recognition so that their Father is glorified by their efforts. Isn't that beautiful?

There are times that recognition comes even to a Servant Leader when their work is noticed by others, and the Servant Leader should be grateful for the work the Lord has allowed through them, giving all the glory and credit to their Heavenly Father. When was the last time you did something that you knew truly mattered?

- Perhaps you sat with a loved one during their final moments on this earth. You were their peace and calm amidst the unknown moments they were facing. It Matters! They may have been incoherent, but the body absorbs energy, and the ear hears until the last breath is drawn so your time was well spent. We never have such a beautiful opportunity to serve someone we love so selflessly like that again, serving them in the darkest hours of their life is special and from a place of love and compassion. It matters!
- Maybe you complimented the waitress for her service, and she nearly teared up in appreciation for how you noticed her because she was having a difficult shift that day. It matters!
- What about the man who is always strait laced, and poker faced that you made smile one day because you shared one of your smiles with him. It matters!
- Helping a child who made a spill and telling them it's ok instead of yelling at them. It matters!
- Raising a soft gentle hand to an animal that has been abused. It matters!

- Putting an arm around a friend who is hurting without trying to fix their problems or lecture them. It matters!

We must never underestimate the power of a kind word or expression to someone you know or towards complete strangers. It may be the only kind word or gesture they've had all day. It seems that the whole world has their heads buried in their cell phones; when they're walking, at family meals, during movies and family activities, at work, while driving. If we take but a moment to look someone in the eye, to speak to them, to smile at them, to throw our hand up and wave as we pass by them - imagine for a moment - the impact these acts of kindness could make. These small moments make a huge impact! It all matters!

Who We're Created to Be

Servant Leadership can look different for everyone. It's easy to forget that we have the power to serve others in such a way that everything we do impacts the life of someone else. Why then do we stay in this cycle of serving ourselves and our own selfish motives? I believe that we are all created equal in the image of God Almighty and His Divine spirit resides within us from the moment of conception in our mother's womb. Scripture tells us in Jeremiah 1:5 "Before I formed you in the womb I knew you, before you were born, I set you apart; I appointed you as a prophet to the nations."

We aren't placed upon this earth by chance. We are divinely appointed to come and serve a purpose greater than ourselves. Psalm 139:13-14 tell us: "For you created my inmost being you knit me together in my mother's womb. I praise you because I am fearfully and wonderfully made; your works are wonderful; I know that full well." You see, God put each one of us on this Earth for a purpose and it's our duty to discover what our purpose is and to fulfill the plan He has for our lives. Believe it or not, it's not as difficult to figure out the plan for our life if we let go of the reins and allow the Lord to lead us. That's what Servant Leadership is all about. Releasing the control and allowing the Lord to use us for His purpose and for His glory.

I was raised by a Servant Leader; God rest his sweet soul. My father was the type of man who would give the shirt off his back, he would give you the last dime he had to his name, he would feed you before he would feed himself and he shared the love of Jesus with everyone he met. Now this man had his flaws as we all do and he wasn't a saint by any means; however, his Servant Leadership example laid a strong foundation for who I would become. He led by example how we should love others and serve them. He also had his moments of exemplifying quite the opposite, but this too is par for the course. In his later years he would load up horses and wagons, piles and piles of clothing and shoes, grills and coolers full of food supplies. He would visit the very places that he once frequented to buy illegal street drugs. He'd bring food to feed the physical hunger of these people, clothing to fulfill their tangible needs and he'd preach the word of God to spiritually feed their souls. This is Servant Leadership at its rawest form. Matthew 25:35-40 says, "For I was hungry, and you gave me food, I was thirsty and you gave me drink, I was a stranger and you welcomed me, I was naked and you clothed me, I was sick and you visited me, I was in prison and you came to me. Truly I tell you, whatever you did for one of the least of these brothers and sisters of mine, you did for me."

Having a father with such a legacy and impactful testimony certainly made way for the type of leader I'd become as an adult. I believe the Lord prepares us for the calling He will place on our life, and He allows us to have experiences to prepare us for where he is leading us. It may not always be butterflies and rainbows; oftentimes it's salt and vinegar but these experiences and hardships are the very ground from which He can build us up from. Just like a diamond is created under great pressure so too are we as gems for Christ. It's been in those moments of despair and rock-bottom places that I have grown the most in my walk with Christ and He's used those moments to equip me with His armor for the work He's called me to.

If I were being honest, I wouldn't choose Servant Leadership in my right mind as the path for my life. It's exhausting - mentally, physically and emotionally draining, it causes spiritual warfare and daily battles and struggles and quite frankly it's difficult for people to understand me. I've always had labels such as "you're sweet", "you're too nice", "you're a doormat for people to walk on", "people will run all over you", "kindness is mistaken for weakness", "you've got to toughen up", "grow thicker skin", "you're a pushover", "they'll take advantage of you", and so many other labels and harsh words have been thrown at me from as far back as I can recall; even in childhood. Yet I've remained true to myself despite it.

I believe that I was born with a sweet, meek, kind, loving and gentle spirit. My father's choices and examples laid before me made an impact on who I am engrained to be. My faith over the years has remained constant and steady. The Lord knew what His plan for my life would be. Jeremiah 29:11 "For I know the plans I have for you says the Lord, plans to prosper you to give you hope and a future."

Lead By Example

Our Heavenly Father IS a Servant Leader. He modeled for us how we should live our lives, and He equips us with everything we need to carry out His plan for our lives. If only more folks would step into their calling and lead through serving others rather than serving themselves. I don't always get it right; I make plenty of mistakes, but praise God I serve a loving father who forgives me and has grace sufficient for all my needs.

Jesus led by example and the Bible is filled with scriptures that remind us of our call to serve. We're called to love like Jesus and live our life from the example he set for us. Just as we are commanded to serve others, scripture also reveals to us that our efforts aren't without reward.

- Mark 10:45 - "For even the Son of Man did not come to be served, but to serve, and to give his life as a ransom for many."
- Matthew 5:16 - "In the same way, let your light shine before others, that they may see your good deeds and glorify your Father in heaven."
- 1 Peter 4:10 - "Each of you should use whatever gift you have received to serve others, as faithful stewards of God's grace in its various forms."
- Luke 6:38 - "Give, and it will be given to you. A good measure, pressed down, shaken together and running over, will be poured into your lap. For with the measure you use, it will be measured to you."

- 2 Chronicles 15:7 - "But as for you, be strong and do not give up, for your work will be rewarded."

Christ's example and Biblical confirmations through His written word lays a foundation from which we can grow upon. How amazing it is that we have a loving Heavenly Father, the Savior of the world to model how we should live our lives and fulfill His plan and purpose.

Looking Back

As I reflect upon my life thus far and the choices I've made, the lives I've encountered, the paths I took; I can't help but realize that I've left my mark in Servant Leadership along my journey. I think of the years I spent in the private sector climbing the ladder in banking. I had the opportunity to be an appointed leader through management positions that gave me my first encounters with Servant Leadership. At that time, I doubt I'd ever heard of Servant Leadership or had any realization that it was at play in my journey. However, looking back I can see where my leadership with serving others left a mark.

As an employee, leader, colleague, friend in the workplace I strive to improve the working conditions for everyone in my work circle. I learn and cross train on everything possible to be able to support my colleagues in times of higher volume, I'd support the manager in their goals and try to improve their outcomes in anyway I could, as a supervisor I'd encourage and support my team patiently teaching them their role and reward them with incentives to keep their motivation going. I realize now that my work ethics and my leadership style is vastly different than that of many others in the same positions or roles. I have this untamed desire to learn, develop, grow, cross train and deeply understand my workplace, the company, the processes and the reasons why we do the things we do and how the processes work. I've always been one to question things no one else would ever question or to challenge a process if there seemed to be a simpler way. My style has brought me many challenges along the way and has caused me undue distress because others simply don't have the same mindset and curiosity that I have. I have no regrets, however, because of my curiosity and questioning I've seen procedures transform and processes change for the better of the company, employees and customers.

In my teaching career, Servant Leadership was a major part of my role. Children need a leader, a coach, a listening ear, a compassionate heart, an empathetic mindset and grace. It was in education that I saw my Servant Leadership in action. I was more than a classroom teacher to the students, parents and colleagues. I was someone they could trust, confide in, come to at their darkest hour, count on to have their back, a source of encouragement and empowerment and so much more. I had relationships with students, colleagues and parents unlike many others in the same profession. I was told countless times how I was "just different" than any other teacher they ever met before. I can't take any credit for this; I owe it all to the Lord who created me and gave me the spirit within me to be set apart to make a difference.

Education is a scary place in the 21st century! Students and staff feel afraid to come to school for all the tragedies we've heard of, the drills and emergency preparations we must train for and the threats that come in that challenges the safety and well-being of everyone. Vigilance is critical and the best way to be vigilant with students is to know them, know their parents and be involved in their life beyond the walls of the classroom. To this day former students contact me, run up to me in public if they see me and former parents still reach out to inquire about my wellbeing and whereabouts. This connection to people doesn't happen without intentionality. It took endless hours of commitment to build relationships with students and their families. What better way to gain the dedication of a student in your classroom than to genuinely care about them and for them and to be connected to their guardians who also care for them?

It was in the classroom that I:

- saw students come out of shells they had never been brave enough to escape from
- witnessed students' creativity come alive again in an age of technology and lost arts and abstract thinking
- watched as lightbulbs came on when students grasped a typically difficult concept to understand – lightbulb moments were the best
- empowered students to search themselves for dreams and aspirations they had never considered before and then helped them map out a plan to achieve them
- motivated students who were so far in a hole of pity that they didn't do any of their work or participate in any of their classes; I've seen them come back from all F's to passing with flying colors
- lead students in building their vision of a business and bring it to life through art and creativity

- supported students in their future endeavors like scholarships, letters of recommendation, internships and many others

This list isn't exhaustive of all the things I witnessed as a Servant Leader in the classroom, this just brushes the surface. I look back now and am amazed at the incredible impact my years of education service must have made. I started teaching Fall of 2020, the year of C-19. We were in masks, more remote than on campus and it was a scary time for students as well as adults. We had 10-day quarantines, and every cough or sneeze had to be checked for the virus. Education during that time took a major hit and our kids are still digging out of the holes those years caused. Entering education during such a pivotal time in our history was brave to say the least on my part. To this day I don't know how I went from a master's in accounting straight into teaching high school business classes and getting my license to teach. Today, it really makes no sense to me. At the time I was in the trenches of teaching full time and in school part time to get my teaching degree while a single mom with two small children.

Looking back, I can see how those steps in my journey were perfectly orchestrated to serve a purpose and plan larger than the need for an income or my desire to teach. I see now that I was placed in education at the exact moment that kids needed someone with compassion and empathy more than ever. They needed a leader who didn't have all the answers but was willing to go to bat for them and find out the answer. They needed a maternal figure to nurture their frightened hearts through a very dark time in our world. I was in education long enough to see the transition from fully masked to masked only when required to be by the CDC to returning to a new normal of sorts without masks. I witnessed the kids who stayed masked beyond the requirement to "hide" from their reality to "mask" their identity, to "quiet" their voice. I vividly recall the students who dropped their mask during their time in my classroom. Call it happenstance if you wish but I fully believe it was the love and compassion of a teacher who genuinely cared for and saw them beyond their mask and could identify their hidden identity.

It was during those 4 critical years in education that I saw the fruits of my labor. Josh Shipp said, "every kid is one caring adult away from being a success story". I lived out that quote like it was my job in the classroom. I felt the honor, privilege and duty to be that one positive caring adult to every child that walked in my classroom. As with all things in life, we can't win them all, but I'd say I had a majority won over by being myself and authentically meeting the kids where they were with an empathetic ear, compassionate heart, warm embrace and positive word of encouragement.

Looking Ahead

Many great authors, including Chris Gardner and Shakespeare have used the quote "The world is your oyster, it's up to you to find the pearls". My string of pearls is abundant, and my work here is not yet finished. I have opportunities to continue this work as a Servant Leader, leaving a mark of compassion and love upon all those who I have the pleasure of encountering. I won't always have supporters and admirers and I've seen my share of haters over the years and to this day I have folks in my circle that are intimidated by my personality and God given spirit. I'll continue to seek my Father's will upon my life and heed His calling to fulfill His purpose and plan for my life. I've embraced the challenge and commitment this calling on my life asks of me.

There's a reason that our rearview mirror is so small; what lies behind us pales in comparison to what's to come. When I look back, I can see all these small glimpses of impact and sprinkles of love like confetti in the lives I've encountered. Looking ahead, the future is like the front windshield – full of opportunities, choices, obstacles, mountains, valleys and an ocean full of oysters with endless pearls to be found. When I look ahead, I see promise and hope.

There's a sense of peace knowing that if we're doing the work of the Lord then that's the only work, we must do. There will be setbacks, disappointments, failures, obstacles, hurdles to cross and difficult people to encounter along the way. This is how the pearls are formed. It takes a grain of sand inside of the oyster to cause irritation then the oyster secretes nacre to coat the irritant protecting the muscle from it. The formation of a pearl can takes six months to four years. I'm amazed at this specific timeline and the timelines of the pearls I can reflect having harvested in my life. It seems that each time a pearl was harvested in my life it was about a four-year span in the process. My education pearl was created in exactly four years' time.

I have a great sense of encouragement after reflecting upon my experiences as a Servant Leader and the possibilities and opportunities to continue this work that lies before me.

Blessings To You

May this chapter encourage you to connect with your inner Servant Leader. Thank you for spending time with me gaining my perspective of Servant Leadership. May the Lord bless you and keep you and place Servant Leaders in your life when you need them. As difficult as it may be, accept the service others bestow upon you graciously and always give of yourself generously, for every act of kindness matters! Servant Leadership matters!

Servant Leadership Reflections

1. A New Year has just begun, resolutions are well underway, perhaps your resolutions are going to plan or maybe you're like me and you didn't make any this year because in years past they seem to fizzle out. I challenge you to create a promise to yourself today that will help you reach the life you wish to live. Perhaps you have an addiction to lie down, you may have resentment to clear up, maybe you're holding onto grief that is wreaking havoc on your progress. I urge you to use the blank space provided to write your thoughts and make yourself a promise to work on the area that is holding you back from the blessings that await you in 2025.

2. Look back for a moment and reflect upon the "pearls" in your life and list them below:

_____
_____
_____
_____
_____
_____
_____
_____
_____
_____

3. What "pearls" do you wish to create in the next 6 months of this new year?

_____
_____
_____
_____
_____
_____
_____
_____
_____
_____

4. Look even further ahead and think about the "pearls" you wish to manifest in the next four years. You may not know exactly their composition or how you'll create them but think about the habits, routines, and ways in which you could prepare yourself to produce pearls long term.

_____
_____
_____
_____
_____
_____
_____
_____

5. Write gratitude in the space below for someone who has modeled Servant Leadership in your life, what they did, how it made you feel and what impact it had upon your life.

_____
_____
_____
_____
_____
_____
_____
_____
_____

Pray with me please:

Dear Heavenly Father,

I want to thank you for setting the divine example of Servant Leadership before us.

Thank you for placing people in our journey to share their leadership and compassion with us. Lord, thank you for the qualities you've gifted to me to walk in your authority as a Servant Leader and work within me to further develop these skills. Empower me to embrace your call upon my life and help me manifest the blessings you have for me. I pray for your guidance and support in creating the "pearls" of my life that it may bring honor and glory to you and leave a lasting imprint on this cold and dark world in which we live. Thank you for this. I love you Lord Jesus and praise you for all that you are, and I thank you for all that you've done and all you plan to do.

It's in your name, Jesus, we ask these things.

Amen.

AUTHOR BIOGRAPHY
Natalie Martin

Natalie Martin is passionate about transformative leadership and the power of servant leadership to inspire and uplift individuals and organizations. Natalie has a unique background that blends the worlds of banking and public education. With over 14 years of experience in the banking industry, Natalie has cultivated a deep understanding of leadership, financial services, and team development. This experience, combined with a career in the public education sector, has reinforced the importance of empathy, collaboration, and service to others as central principles of effective leadership.

Throughout her career, Natalie has been driven by a commitment to making a positive impact both personally and professionally. She has witnessed firsthand the profound impact that servant leadership can have on creating sustainable success and fostering meaningful relationships. Her journey has led to a profound belief that true leadership involves empowering and uplifting those around you, whether in the classroom or the corporate boardroom.

Through her writing, Natalie aims to empower leaders at all levels to adopt a service-oriented mindset, emphasizing empathy, humility, and the importance of putting others' needs first.

Her approach is to inspire others to embrace servant leadership as a transformative approach to achieving personal growth, organizational success, and a meaningful contribution to society.

When not writing, speaking, or planning her next collaboration, Natalie enjoys spending quality time with her family, friends and church family. She also enjoys painting, spending time with her pets and taking weekend getaways supporting local towns and small businesses. Her desire towards self-improvement is never exhausted as Natalie seeks opportunities to grow, learn, and serve in every area of life. To inquire about Natalie speaking for your organization NataliePowell81@yahoo.com.

REFLECTING ON LIFE'S JOURNEY: EMBRACING A LEGACY

By Jaclyn Michelle Nagle

REFLECTING ON LIFE'S JOURNEY: EMBRACING A LEGACY

As I reached the milestone age of 50, I found myself contemplating the legacy I would leave behind. The absence of biological children or grandchildren who shared my DNA made me ponder this deeply. In discussing this with my husband, he reassured me that my legacy would be evident through the lives I have touched throughout the years. This endorsement led me to reflect on my past and how it has shaped my vision for the future.

When I was about five years old, I distinctly remember sitting in my kindergarten class, passionately sharing my dream of becoming a teacher. It may be a common aspiration for five-year-olds, yet I realized many adults might overlook such dreams, dismissing them as mere childhood fancy. However, my classroom was not typical; I was enrolled in a special education school due to being born with cerebral palsy. This environment was the ideal setting for receiving the necessary physical and occupational therapy every day, as was recommended in the late 1970s.

That year marked a significant shift when I learned I would be "mainstreamed" into the regular education system. This development was short-lived owing to surgery on my legs, which required me to be in casts for two to three months, necessitating a return to the special education school. Despite these setbacks, my teacher was committed to continuing the regular school curriculum to prevent me from falling behind. Recognizing my burgeoning desire to educate, she gave me opportunities to read stories and conduct activities with my classmates—this was my inaugural experience in serving others.

Servant leadership often involves sharing power within a group. As someone with a disability, I was driven to empower others to meet their full potential. My upbringing was not particularly religious, yet I inherently knew that serving others was integral to my faith and what God expected of me. People often explained my disability as God's way of designating a special purpose for me. My youthful interpretation of this was that my mission was to educate, particularly those with disabilities.

My aspiration to become a teacher remained unwavering through my schooling years. Post-graduation, I enrolled in a well-regarded "teacher's college" determined to pursue a career in special education. My disability was never a hindrance, thanks to the equality in treatment I enjoyed alongside my siblings. However, upon entering the professional realm, I faced my first encounter with discrimination due to my disability.

Initially, my college application stated my intent to become an elementary school teacher rather than specializing in special education. I had to officially alter my major for which meeting with the Dean of the special education faculty was mandatory. Progressing through two years of college meant my prerequisites were fulfilled by then. Unfortunately, a bout of pneumonia coincided with my scheduled appointment with the Dean and attempts to reschedule were met with the stipulation that missing the meeting would delay my major change by a semester. Determined not to pause my education, I attended the meeting as planned.

Staying in My Purpose

When I reflect on the challenging meeting with the Dean, I recall feeling vulnerable yet determined. Recovering from pneumonia at the time, I was left with little voice to argue my case. The Dean questioned my desire to change my major, and I shared the deep motivation to help others. However, her response was discouraging, claiming someone like me could never handle a classroom full of children. I countered with confidence, explaining that with a well-structured classroom, the need to chase kids around was unnecessary. Unfortunately, her disbelief in my capabilities saw no end, as she pointed to my diminished voice as evidence of my incompatibility with teaching. That day marked my first encounter with feeling defeated due to my disability.

Despite this setback, I was determined not to leave college abruptly. I shifted focus, changing my major to English with a specialization in writing. The head of disability services expressed relief over my decision, adding that individuals with disabilities can sometimes overestimate what they can achieve in college. Her remarks only served to deepen my anguish. In the pursuit of coping, I made hasty decisions like overloading myself with classes, leading to burnout and eventual withdrawal from college due to mental health challenges.

The road to recovery was far from straightforward. For over a year, I confined myself to my apartment, engaging in activities like watching TV, surfing the Internet, and working remotely. During this period, I secured a job with AOL, launching and overseeing a disability support chat, and contributed to disability community bulletin boards.

Working within the disability community was not new to me. At 17, I discovered a groundbreaking independent living center in my community and began volunteering there during the summer transition from high school to college. They extended a peer mentoring position to me, which I declined, steadfast in my dream of becoming a teacher. My experiences at community college revealed a supportive educational environment with a manageable pace, unlike traditional four-year institutions.

After a year and a half in seclusion, a profound change occurred. I can only attribute this shift to divine intervention, as if God were gently reminding me of my greater purpose. As John 13:15 affirms, *"I have set you an example that you should do as I have done for you."* This scripture resonated deeply, compelling me to exemplify resilience and service in my journey.

Though teaching seemed improbable, I discovered a different avenue to serve: an associate's degree in human services at a local community college. Optimism and uncertainty mingled as I embarked on this new academic journey just three days post-surgery. Doubts about my ability to succeed lingered, yet I found myself excelling and even took on tutoring in English. Each achievement built my confidence, though a fear of further setbacks never fully subsided.

An Inspirational Journey: From Intern to Executive Director

In my last year at community college, I embarked on a journey that would profoundly shape my career and personal growth. Fresh off an internship at an agency, I found myself reminiscing about my volunteer experience at another agency after high school graduation. Driven by this memory, I reached out and inquired about internship opportunities. To my delight, they welcomed me onboard. This turned out to be more than just an internship; it was a pivotal moment in my life, one that some might call divine intervention.

During this initial internship, I immersed myself in the agency's various services and discovered how these services could benefit me personally. As the internship drew to a close, I faced the requirement of completing a second internship. After consulting with agency staff and my professor, we concluded that I could continue at the same agency but contribute to a different department.

The independent living department, where most services were provided directly to consumers, soon became my new workspace. Following the dismissal of a peer counselor, the department director requested my assistance in managing her caseload. This involved verifying the well-being of clients, many of whom were families requiring support for their children's individualized educational plans. The job entailed much more than previously thought, and it became clear that there was a significant need for peer counseling. With this realization, I dove into the peer counseling manual and began counseling as many people as I could manage with the time I had. To my surprise, my efforts were recognized when the director offered me the role of peer counselor upon graduation.

This role allowed me to blend my desire to help others and fulfill a sense of purpose. Though not teaching, it was an opportunity to serve others. I began part-time, eventually expanding the program into a full-time position. Over time, my responsibilities shifted. I transitioned from peer mentoring to working with youth with disabilities, supporting their transition from high school to adulthood. I became an educational advocate, striving for inclusive education within regular school districts, as separate schools were phased out but the need for support services persisted. I dedicated 22 years to this agency before feeling that my chapter there had ended, especially following the unpredictable post-COVID world.

Subsequently, I took a position at another agency for seven months. However, a long-standing aspiration remained unfulfilled: becoming a director. In May 2022, an unexpected phone call from an old friend presented me with an opportunity. She inquired if I was interested in the Executive Director position at a similar agency in a different location. Initially, I thought it was a joke, but she assured me it was genuine. I submitted my resume and references more to appease her than myself, but within two days, I was called for an interview.

This opportunity was particularly special because I had previously applied to the same agency years ago but was not selected. The first interview, with the selection committee, ended with a promise of updates regardless of the outcome. While I felt the interview went well, my expectations were tempered by past experiences. To my astonishment, they called me back for a second interview. Something within me—perhaps divine intervention—prompted me to attend. By the end of the day, hope had sparked anew as I received a call offering me the position. After 22 years, while it wasn't the teaching position I had initially envisioned, this role embodied my dream job. It allowed me to impact the disability community, a cause deeply meaningful to me.

As I reflect on this path—from an intern seeking direction to an Executive Director with a renewed sense of purpose—I am filled with awe and gratitude. It's a testament to the power of perseverance, faith, and readiness to seize opportunities that align with one's values and passions.

Serving Others and Leaving a Legacy

My new journey had begun. Blessed with an opportunity to serve others in the disability community, I embarked on a path where my passion and profession seamlessly intertwined. While working at different agencies, I completed my master's degree in organizational leadership and began my doctorate studies in leadership. Leadership, particularly servant leadership, is a style that resonates deeply with me. For me, it's more than just a method; it's a calling to serve others so they can see God's grace shining through my actions.

Though not every day is filled with sunshine and rainbows, we advocate tirelessly through the storms to make this world a better place. Shortly after accepting my new position, I turned 50—a milestone that prompted reflection. Would people remember me when I'm gone? What would my legacy be? These questions haunted me, swirling in my mind and bringing me to tears.

In this period of introspection, I questioned whether I was fulfilling God's work and what I could leave behind. Though I have bonus daughters, nieces I consider daughters, and a few cherished people, I feared they might not remember me. Unlike biological family ties, I couldn't pass down tangible heirlooms. Such thoughts led to heartfelt discussions with my husband, who reminded me of all the good I bring to the world through God's grace. He was right—I have time to do the work that matters.

I believe DNA doesn't make a family; relationships do. As someone who lives in God's word, I cherish relationships that help build and support one another. It is through these bonds that I can spread God's love and grace. Recently, our community lost four incredible individuals who devoted their lives to advocating for equality and inclusion within the disability community. They will always be remembered for their contributions. I can only hope to be remembered in the same light and for my legacy to continue through those I have served.

Servant Leadership Reflections

1. What legacy do you hope to leave for your loved ones and community?

_____
_____
_____
_____
_____
_____
_____
_____
_____
_____
_____
_____
_____

2. How can you apply principles of servant leadership in your daily life?

_____
_____
_____
_____
_____
_____
_____
_____

3. In what ways do you cultivate meaningful relationships that go beyond genetic ties?

_____
_____
_____
_____
_____
_____
_____
_____
_____

4. What challenges have you faced in trying to create positive change in your community? How did you overcome them?

_____
_____
_____
_____
_____
_____
_____
_____
_____
_____
_____

AUTHOR BIOGRAPHY
Jaclyn Michelle Nagle, MPA, BCEA
Executive Director

Ms. Jaclyn Nagle has been a lifelong disability advocate. Working for a Center for Independent Living (CIL) in Reading PA for many years; her passion was to address education for children with disabilities.

Even before that she started her advocacy with her parents as a child with a disability at a very young age. She was always taught to fight for herself, she did, and then as she matured fought the hard fight for others. Currently she has been at our CIL since June 2022, and has made outstanding strides like this organization has never seen before. She is by far our best Executive Director in the history of the Disability Empowerment Center (DEC). She is determined that staff train on advocacy immediately upon hire. advocacy, where in the past we were admonished for doing so, as past EDs never understood what we did or what a CIL was developed to do. In her short time with DEC she has spoken in public numerous times at universities, churches, private businesses and other entities. She is very organized and educates the staff about advocacy and other duties to assist consumers with disabilities. All done, without concern of her (dis)abilities, she pushes on with energy and optimism, and encouragement for all the staff and Board members.

"We are so ecstatic that she decided to accept her position. I must say, even as our center begins to grow, our staff under Jaclyn is a close family supporting each other at every turn. It is a wonderful place to work, and we know we have her support. She makes it easy to adequately, effectively, and kindly get our advocacy efforts accepted throughout our communities. We serve two counties in PA currently, and hope to grow to serve everyone who needs our assistance. We are so blessed to have her in charge of our organization."

To reach out to Jaclyn about speaking for your organization please contact her at jnagle@decpa.org or at 717.394.1890 as this is a passion for her to share with others leadership, team work and resilience strategies.

LEGACY OF LEADERSHIP: THE 5C FRAMEWORK FOR SERVING OTHERS

By Cindy Craig Hall

LEGACY OF LEADERSHIP: THE 5C FRAMEWORK FOR SERVING OTHERS

Small Town Beginnings

Bassett, Virginia, is more than just a small town nestled in the foothills of the Blue Ridge Mountains; it was the backdrop of my formative years. With our home 30 minutes from the nearest grocery store, each trip to "town" was an adventure, often passing iconic furniture companies like Bassett Furniture and Hooker Furniture. The quaint charm of Bassett's Main Street was always bustling, and the rhythmic clattering of passing trains became a metaphor for my journey—steadily moving forward and striving for growth. I enjoyed the time waiting for the train to pass, wondering where it was coming from and going to.

My family's ties to the furniture industry run deep. My paternal grandfather, Emory Craig, retired from the Bassett Table Plant, and my maternal grandmother, whom I called Granny, worked as a secretary for J. Clyde Hooker, Sr., keeping a cherished Hooker bedroom set from 1954 until her passing in 2017. I have fond memories of sleeping in that bedroom during my visits. My great-grandfather, Walter Franklin Spicer, crafted by hand beautiful grandfather clocks. I hope to own one of the two still in our family. We shared a special bond through our birthday on March 4, and he sent me a dollar for every year I lived, a gesture I thought was so cool, although my younger siblings did not.

Growing up during the furniture and textiles boom, I always felt drawn to these fields. I admired Granny, who worked as a customer service representative for J & J Southeast Container, which supplied corrugated boxes to these industries. I loved to watch her get dressed up for work and listen to stories about her customers. She loved taking care of whatever they needed to make their business run smoothly. Her extraordinary life has shaped my own, and I realize now that I've modeled much of who I am after her.

My Granny: A Pillar of Strength and Legacy

Granny married young, and my grandfather, Leff Vaughn Royal, returned from World War II to finish high school, where he met her as her bus driver. They fell in love and had my mother, Brenda Jean, in 1948. Shortly after, he was called back for the Korean War, serving as a Sergeant First Class in the Army infantry. He was missing in action in November 1950 and received multiple awards, including a Purple Heart and Bronze Star.

When a local policeman delivered the tragic news, Granny became a widow at just 21, with a two-year-old. She moved back in with her parents in Galax, VA, and attended Perry Business School to learn secretarial skills. A few years later, she met my step-grandfather, Hender Saul, a rockabilly musician, and they welcomed my aunt Connie in 1955. Granny worked as a secretary at Hooker Furniture and other companies before finding her favorite job at J&J Southeast Container in 1963.

After over 20 years of marriage, she lost Hender to a massive heart attack at 45, becoming a widow again at 45. Even though I was young, I admired her resilience as she worked hard, paid off her house, and retired at 59. Inspired by her financial independence, I began contributing to my 401K at 21 after she encouraged me to save consistently and be generous.

Granny loved to travel. For my 21st birthday, we flew to Orlando, as a reward for rolling her coins. Her adventurous spirit led her to amazing trips to Europe and many cruises. After her passing in 2017, I learned just how big her heart was. Granny was very generous to neighbors, friends, family, and our church. If she saw a need, she would quietly take care of it.

Her legacy taught me the value of hard work, commitment, resilience, and being ready to help others. I am grateful for the 50 years I had with her and strive to honor her memory by embodying her generous spirit.

Stepping into the Workforce

After graduating high school, I had set a goal to work in an office like my Granny. Inspired by her success, I enrolled at Patrick Henry Community College in Martinsville, Virginia, pursuing an associate degree in Information Technology. While waiting for class one day, I spotted a job posting for a part-time position in the Computer Department at Hooker Furniture. I applied and met my first mentor, Charlene Bowling, who would later become one of the company's first female Vice Presidents.

I started my job on August 3, 1987, and was thrilled to meet Clyde Hooker that day. I had heard so much about him from my Granny, who had worked for his father in the 1950s. It was surprising and heartwarming that he took time to meet me, a part-time employee.

However, the next morning, I woke up sick with strep throat and missed two days of work. I was anxious about what this would mean for my job. To my astonishment, when I returned that Thursday, Clyde checked on me just minutes after I arrived.

This act of kindness was not an act at all, it was how Clyde was every day and to everyone. This experience was one that I have never truly gotten over. This was the first time I had been exposed in the workplace to what a good leader looks like. I was blessed to be able to watch Clyde Hooker model servant leadership at a young age and have mentorship from Charlene to help shape my early career.

Lessons from Granny and Clyde Hooker

Clyde Hooker, Jr. was born on December 20, 1920, and passed away on July 12, 2010. His loss deeply affected everyone, especially those at the Corporate Office. As the saying goes, it's not the dates that matter, but the "dash" in between. Clyde made every second of that dash count, leaving a lasting impact that endures even 14 years later.

Clyde's father, Clyde Hooker, Sr, started Hooker Furniture in 1924. Clyde Jr. sat on his shoulders at 4 years old and pulled the whistle to start the first day of production. After graduating from Virginia Military Institute, he served as a Second Lieutenant in the 752nd Field Artillery Battalion during World War II, earning the Bronze Star and four campaign stars before being discharged as a Captain in 1946.

Returning to Martinsville, Clyde immersed himself in the business, first learning manufacturing and then sales. He rose to Sales Manager in 1956 and became President in 1960, serving until 1988, and remained involved as Chairman and CEO until late 2000. Even in his final years, despite declining eyesight, he would still greet people with a warm hug and a whistle.

Just like my Granny's commitment to her family and community, Clyde was deeply committed to the furniture industry, his community, and most importantly, the people at Hooker Furniture. If you spoke to 100 people who knew him, you'd hear words like humility, integrity, intelligence, motivating, kindness, and generosity—qualities that truly defined him. These are a few things that Granny and Clyde had in common.

1C. Commitment

Clyde's Commitment

Clyde Hooker was deeply committed to his employees and shareholders, ensuring everyone felt valued and necessary for the company's success. As a Hooker employee, I wanted to make him proud, giving my all every day. It wasn't just me; everyone felt the same way.

In my early 20s, I worked in Customer Service and often joined Clyde on factory visits. I marveled at how he knew everyone's name, greeted them with warmth, and inquired about their families by their first name. During furniture markets, he did the same with customers, remembering their sales numbers and offering genuine support, especially if they had faced challenges. His ability to connect with each person was truly inspiring.

Though I don't possess Clyde's remarkable memory, I strive to make others feel special and important, just as he did. Recently, while working at a local manufacturing facility in North Carolina, I learned as many names as possible, engaged with employees about their favorite sports teams, and checked in on their families.

I may not be Clyde Hooker, but his example taught me the importance of caring and respecting everyone's contributions. I'm grateful for the lessons I learned from him; they've enriched my life and hopefully touched those around me as well.

Granny's Commitment

My Granny exemplified compassion and empathy throughout her life. As a hospice volunteer for 30 years, she was dependable, faithful to the mission, and helped support families facing their most challenging moments with unwavering dedication. Beyond that, she cared for my mother for 17 years until her passing in 2017. My Mom's health struggles began when she was 40, with a benign tumor wrapped around her spinal cord. At 20, I was learning to navigate these challenges alongside my younger brother and sister, while my mom underwent a long recovery. With perseverance and months of physical therapy, she learned to walk again and returned to work. Unfortunately, the tumor recurred 11 years later, leading to a heartbreaking reality: this time, the damage was too severe for her to fully recover.

My Dad, another hero in this story, has been her devoted caregiver for over 25 years. Granny felt this loss deeply; seeing her child in pain was a burden she carried. Yet, she was my mom's best friend, visiting three times a week to wash and curl her hair, work on puzzles, and simply be present. Granny's commitment to my mom's well-being, despite her inability to change the situation, was truly inspiring. It reflected a profound love and commitment wrapped in compassion—a legacy I deeply admire, alongside my dad's enduring love and dedication.

2C. Collaboration

Paul Toms, President of Hooker Furniture until a few years ago, shares how Clyde Hooker balanced decisiveness with empowerment. While he made tough calls, when necessary, Clyde fostered an environment where employees felt free to make their own decisions without fear of reprimand. If someone's choice didn't pan out, he'd simply ask, "What do we do next?" This approach cultivated a culture of collaboration and acceptance, leading to better ideas and teamwork.

One of Clyde's memorable sayings was, "When you're in a foxhole and getting shot at, do something. If it doesn't work, do something else." This mindset encouraged creative problem-solving and collaboration across the organization. Clyde celebrated the big wins when new ideas, concepts, or processes were developed by cross-functioning groups in the organization.

Collaboration is one of my core principles, as I believe that many minds are better than one. It not only leads to more thoughtful solutions but also creates a sense of belonging, empowering everyone to contribute. Working together towards a common goal is not only rewarding but also brings a sense of ownership to all involved. The process brings fun to work together for a common purpose and to allow everyone to think outside of the box. It is rewarding for all and gives everyone involved a sense of ownership in the project and company.

Facing Personal Tragedy

In 1997, Mike and I faced a heart-wrenching loss when we learned that our baby had a rare and fatal birth defect called anencephaly at just 24 weeks into my pregnancy. It was a devastating time, but what stood out most was the incredible support I received from Clyde, my co-workers, and the entire Hooker team. Their compassion truly made a difference during those dark days. I still treasure the handwritten letter Clyde sent me. It was heartfelt and sincere, encouraging me to be strong and to take all the time I needed to heal, both physically and mentally. This was classic Clyde—always knowing just the right thing to say, filled with genuine empathy.

3C. Compassion

At the age of 29, I realized how profoundly Clyde's kindness shaped my perspective on leadership and human connection. The compassion he showed me during my family's tragedy has stayed with me, fueling my desire to extend the same kindness to others I've managed or worked with. He instilled in us the importance of caring for one another and being sensitive to what others might be going through.

Clyde had a unique way of brightening the office atmosphere. You could always tell when he was nearby by the cheerful sound of his whistling. He would make his weekly rounds to ask how we were doing, inquire about our families, and share updates on what the company was working on. Those visits felt like special moments, akin to a warm hug from a favorite uncle, and we were always left with smiles on our faces.

As I grew in my role and took on more responsibilities, Clyde would share more in-depth information about the company's direction and challenges. This level of trust was empowering; it made me feel valued and motivated me to contribute to the company's success. We all wanted to make Clyde proud because he believed in us and made us feel like we were part of something meaningful.

Clyde's legacy of compassion and kindness continues to inspire me, reminding me that in leadership, it's essential to nurture the human connections that strengthen our teams. His approach to leadership taught me that true success lies in how we treat one another.

4C. Community

During Clyde Hooker's leadership, the workplace felt like a close-knit family—an experience I've rarely encountered in my 35-year career. This sense of community was both intentional and organic. Back then, our smaller office allowed us to truly connect and support one another through good times and bad. Clyde led by example, taking the time to check in on us almost weekly, sharing laughs and tears. His investment in us forged a group of fierce leaders.

If I gathered those 50 colleagues today, it would take mere seconds for that sense of camaraderie to reignite. Even though some, including Clyde, have passed on or moved on to different careers, our shared respect and love for him endure. The lessons we learned from Clyde stay with us wherever we go, and I feel incredibly blessed to have witnessed such a remarkable culture.

One of my favorite memories is from a Halloween party in 2006 or 2007 when our department dressed as a baseball team. Clyde wanted to join us and dubbed us the "Hooker Honeys." It was a day filled with laughter, fun, and countless photos—a perfect example of the joy he brought to our team.

I strive to embody that same spirit in my leadership. I believe in getting to know my team members—understanding their strengths and weaknesses—and building them up. Authenticity is key; I aim to show my team that I'm human too. Fun should be a part of our success.

In contrast, I once worked under a leader who exemplified the opposite approach. After six months, he still couldn't tell you five things about me. I felt invisible and undervalued, which diminished my productivity and ultimately led me to leave the company after many years. This experience taught me the importance of caring leadership—people want to feel valued and surrounded by a supportive community.

The Role of Creativity in Leadership

5C. Creativity

In Servant Leadership, promoting creativity starts with modeling innovation, and Clyde Hooker was truly exceptional at this. From the beginning of his leadership journey, he understood that for Hooker Furniture to thrive, it needed to stand out. His father's advice to find a niche inspired the company to dive into building entertainment centers in the 1970s. This move transformed Hooker into the go-to brand for entertainment units and wall units, showcasing a commitment to innovation that resonated throughout the industry.

Clyde always emphasized that this success wasn't a solo achievement; it was a collective effort. He would say, "There are no superstars here," reminding everyone that every team member played a crucial role in the company's achievements. This philosophy created an environment where everyone felt valued and empowered to contribute their ideas.

Today's leaders must take this approach further. It's not just about being creative themselves; they need to inspire their teams to embrace creativity in their everyday work. Listening is a fundamental part of this process. The sales representatives, who have direct communication with customers are vital for understanding their needs and desires.

By encouraging open dialogue, leaders can pinpoint problems and opportunities. Collaboration is essential as teams conceptualize ideas, and product development works with engineers to create prototypes. This iterative process, involving customer feedback, ensures the final product meets market needs.

Clyde's legacy reminds us that effective leadership is about building a culture of collaboration and innovation, where every voice matters and creativity flourishes. I have found that leading by example and demonstrating my creative processes can inspire others. I believe incorporating fun into the workplace—through team-building activities and playful brainstorming sessions—energizes the team and transforms the workplace into a vibrant space for innovation and creativity.

The 5C principles seamlessly intertwine in my personal and professional life, enriching my journey as a servant leader.

Commitment drives my dedication to both my family and my colleagues. In my personal life, I strive to be a reliable support system for my husband and friends, prioritizing quality time and being present during their challenges. Similarly, in my professional role, I am committed to empowering my team, ensuring they feel valued and inspired to contribute their best.

Collaboration is a cornerstone of my interactions, whether at home or at work. I foster open communication and shared decision-making with my family, encouraging everyone to express their thoughts and ideas. This collaborative spirit extends to my workplace, where I believe that diverse perspectives lead to innovative solutions. By creating a culture of teamwork, I promote a sense of belonging and ownership among my colleagues.

Compassion is reflected in how I engage with my community and loved ones. Inspired by my Granny, I actively volunteer and support local initiatives, always being sensitive to the struggles of others. This empathy carries into my professional interactions, where I strive to understand and address the needs of my team and clients, ensuring they feel cared for and understood.

Community is vital in both realms of my life. I work to build strong connections with neighbors and friends, fostering an environment of trust and support. In the workplace, I aim to create a family-like atmosphere where everyone feels connected and valued, echoing the sense of belonging I cherish in my personal relationships.

Finally, **Creativity** fuels my passions at home and in my career. I encourage my loved ones to explore their creative pursuits, believing that this enriches our lives and strengthens our bonds. In my professional role, I inspire my team to think outside the box and contribute innovative ideas, transforming our workplace into a vibrant space for growth and collaboration. By integrating these principles into my personal and professional life, I embody the spirit of servant leadership, uplifting those around me and fostering meaningful connections.

Conclusion: The Power of Servant Leadership and a Lasting Legacy

Embracing the 5C's—Commitment, Collaboration, Compassion, Community, and Creativity—has profoundly shaped my path as a servant leader. These principles illuminate my personal and professional interactions, reinforcing the belief that the way we treat one another is essential to creating meaningful connections. Each C enhances the others, creating a comprehensive approach to leadership rooted in genuine care and respect. The lessons imparted by Clyde and my Granny resonate deeply within me.

1. **The Golden Rule**: Treat others as you want to be treated. This principle emphasizes kindness, empathy, and respect in all interactions, as reflected in:

    Matthew 7:12 (NIV): "So in everything, do to others what you would have them do to you."

    Galatians 5:14 (NIV): "For the entire law is fulfilled in keeping this one command: "Love your neighbor as yourself."

2. **Work Hard and Tell the Truth**: Commitment to integrity and hard work is crucial. This is supported by:

    Colossians 3:23 (NIV): "Whatever you do, work at it with all your heart, as working for the Lord, not for human masters."

    Proverbs 11:3 (NIV): "The integrity of the upright guides them, but the unfaithful are destroyed by their duplicity."

3. **Be Humble and Put Others Above Yourself**: Humility is essential in leadership and relationships.

   Philippians 2:3-4 (NIV): "Do nothing out of selfish ambition or vain conceit. Rather, in humility value others above yourselves, not looking to your own interests but each of you to the interests of the others."

   Proverbs 11:2 (NIV): "When pride comes, then comes disgrace, but with humility comes wisdom."

I challenge you to reflect deeply on the power of servant leadership in your own life. Consider how the 5C Framework—Commitment, Collaboration, Compassion, Community, and Creativity—can transform not only your professional endeavors but also your personal relationships.

Ask yourself: Are you truly embodying the principles of kindness, integrity, and humility that honor the legacy of those who inspired you? Just as Clyde and Granny became guiding lights in my life, you too can be that source of inspiration and support for others. In a world that often prioritizes self-interest, dare to stand out by serving others with intentionality and love. Embrace the responsibility of leadership as a calling to uplift those around you, creating ripples of positive change. Let this be the moment you commit to being a beacon of light, reflecting the values that matter most, and inspiring others to do the same.

Servant Leadership Reflections

1. How do you define servant leadership, and in what ways can you integrate it more fully into your professional and personal life?

   _____
   _____
   _____
   _____
   _____
   _____
   _____
   _____

2. In what ways can you apply the Golden Rule—treating others as you wish to be treated—in your daily interactions?

   _____
   _____
   _____
   _____
   _____
   _____
   _____
   _____

3. Reflecting on your current leadership style, where do you see opportunities for greater humility and service to others?

_____
_____
_____
_____
_____
_____
_____
_____
_____
_____

4. What specific actions can you take to show compassion to those around you?

_____
_____
_____
_____
_____
_____
_____
_____
_____
_____
_____

5. How can you inspire others, as Clyde and Granny did for me, to embrace servant leadership in their own lives?

_____
_____
_____
_____
_____
_____
_____
_____

AUTHOR BIOGRAPHY
Cindy Craig Hall

IG: @cindycraighall | LinkedIn: cindycraighall | Facebook: cindycraighall | Email:cindycraighall@gmail.com | Mobile: 276.340.4438

Cindy Hall is a seasoned furniture executive and design consultant with nearly 35 years of experience, including 29 years at Hooker Furnishings and 4 1/2 years at Sherrill Furniture. A two-time recipient of the prestigious ISFD Pinnacle Award, Cindy visionary approach to furniture design and innovation has consistently set her apart. She was also honored as the 2023 Luxe Red Design Award Winner and a finalist for the With-It Mentoring WOW Award in 2021.

Cindy's professional journey includes key leadership roles such as Vice President of Merchandising & Product Development at Sherrill Furniture, Creative Director at The Uttermost Co., and Vice President at Hooker Furnishings. Her work has helped transform countless homes into personalized, functional havens. Cindy had her own breakout capsule collection of one-of-a-kind items called Mélange, which surpassed $20 million in sales over seven years. This success was incredible and significantly changed the company's trajectory. "Pillars of Excellence: 5 Core Principles Framework which guides each project or personal endeavor to success. She enjoys bringing this to sales teams in conference settings, in workshop settings and in roundtable management meetings.

Hall provides professional consulting and is a certified coach also volunteers her time helping women get back on their feet from life-threatening situations so they can thrive in their careers. In addition, she loves to do art and play the piano for her church. Her furniture designs are featured worldwide, and she enjoys learning and applying all aspects of the furniture industry as that is a part of her unique value that she brings to a C-Suite Organization. From her comfortable demeanor to being able to interact with sales teams that lead with customers on the floor to those that are responsible for managing product development and marketing with KPI's to sitting and having coffee with the CEO in a private coaching call Cindy is your basement to the boardroom expert.

Beyond her professional achievements, Cindy is guided in her faith and is dedicated to showing others the love of Jesus, believing He serves as the ultimate example of how we should treat others. She also draws inspiration from two of her role models – her Granny, Juanita Saul, and Clyde Hooker, Jr.

In her spare time, Cindy enjoys traveling and experiencing many different cultures with her husband of 31 years, Mike. Together, they have two sons, Nathan and Logan, and daughter-in-law, Alexis.

To view Cindy's Speaker Media Kit go to her LinkedIn profile.

PEOPLE OF TRANSFORMATION

By Garrett Milby

PEOPLE OF TRANSFORMATION

While watching a lion passing on, Photographer Larry Pannell stated afterwards, *"Life is short. Power is ephemeral. Physical beauty is short-lived, I have seen it in lions. I have seen it in old people. Everyone who lives long enough will become weak and very vulnerable. Therefore, let us be humble. Help the sick, the weak, the vulnerable and most importantly never forget that we will leave the stage one day."*

The passage above invokes a stirring within my soul. To help... While meditating how each of us could/can help. I am left to ponder, what if we were to change the word help to something like serve? Serve the sick, the weak, the vulnerable, etc. What a profound replacement for the word help. To serve, is a great reminder of the greatest servant of all-time; Jesus came not to be served but to serve. Which we are all called to do, SERVE.

I have been blessed. When I say blessed, I mean that I have had so many individuals lean into me and impress upon me what it means to serve. To serve within business organizations, to serve within the community and more importantly to serve their friends and family. In some cases: it was providing a hot meal to a rumbling stomach, providing a warm place to lay one's head. Other times service took the form of providing financially, emotionally, physically or spiritually. Each time though, those individuals would selflessly sacrifice themselves to ultimately help others achieve their needs. At the end of the day, I watched individuals live out The Great Commission serving others and spreading the word of Jesus Christ through words and actions. Simply, I have been blessed. However, I would be remised if I did not take the time to bestow upon you the impact of those individuals and their assistance, as I continue to forge onward as a servant leader.

My only hope is that I capture these grand individuals and their stories of servanthood. In return I hope that it assists you with striving to be the best servant you can be in a day and age where we need more servants than ever before.

Granny

I know that everyone has that one fond family member that they will constantly talk about. The impact that they have on your life stays with you forever. My granny, the glue of our family, was just that to us. Granny was my first example of being a servant, placing service before self in the truest form. She was a lady whom I never saw get too upset or rattled. The calm in the storm and the constant that we all needed when our lives would be falling apart. With her simple words, soft voice she made everything seem at peace. Her smile lit up the room. Her laugh put a smile on your face. Her hugs were of great assurance that everything was going to be alright.

Have you ever heard someone reference a person as "salt of the Earth" that was Brenda Sue. She was one of a kind and I got to call her mine. As a child, while my parents were going through their divorce my granny stepped in and helped raise me and my sister. A grandmother should not have to raise another set of children after rearing her own, but she did without skipping a beat. She always told me, "She would not have had it any other way." As I said, throughout life she was the constant. I always knew granny would be home plate when I needed to recalibrate myself.

As a child granny worked in a factory and I learned so much from her, watching with little eyes. We never went without a hot meal, our clothes were always cleaned, ironed, and neatly put away. Every night she would say prayers with us as her faith was near and dear to her. A memory that stays with me to this day when I hear the old gospel hymns: every Sunday she would have the old country gospel music playing as we got ready for church. Such fond memories. She always ensured we had all we needed along life's journey. Granny instilled so many things in us we probably forgot more things than we ever thanked her for. She did it all not because she had to but because she wanted to. She did it not out of obligation but from a place of love. It was always about love with Granny and being able to serve her family was one of her greatest blessings.

Granny was the truest version of a servant that I ever knew. It did not end with just her family but rolled over into others' as well. She always had an extra plate of food to feed someone or a friend who came home with us, an extra blanket if someone wanted to stay with us. She was just Granny to all who came to know her. She molded us into who we are today and because of her we continue to build upon her legacy as her teachings have been passed on to each generation that comes after her.

The Friend

At the ripe age of twenty-one I was a young adult looking for answers to the thing called life. I had no sense of direction. All I knew was I needed to work to make money, and I found myself working in the warehouse industry. I started my job and after a few weeks working second shift I was afforded the opportunity to switch to first shift. Little did I know that would be one of the best decisions I ever made as it was in that warehouse that

I came across a beautiful soul who I would later refer to as my "second father" enter Joseph Emmanuel Fogle, Joe for short.

One day while at lunch I overheard a person talking about his hometown. Upon hearing where he was from, I could not help but to introduce myself to him. See we grew up only about thirty minutes from each other. Upon our brief discussion a friendship blossomed into a relationship that I am still forever grateful for to this day. It was here over a 16-month friendship that I discovered myself and a passion for becoming something more in life.

As a young adult I had no direction in life. I had no true ambition for anything. I felt worthless honestly. However, it was Joe who invested time and energy into me, that helped mold me into who I am today. Out of all the things I needed at that time in my life Joe "showed up". If I was going to the gym Joe tagged along. If I was going to play basketball after work Joe would be there. As I pondered the next steps in life, Joe was there to listen.

One day at work, I remember this like it was yesterday, Joe said to me "what are you going to do with your life?" I looked at him and I said, I guess I will be like you and make a career here. I was actually amazed that in less than three years on the job I could be making almost $20.00 an hour and in 2004 that was big money. Joe looked at me with the most serious look I have ever seen from him and said "Do not be like me. You are far too talented and smart to spend the rest of your life in a warehouse." He asked, "have you ever entertained the idea of college?" I replied, yes but it cost too much, and I am not sure I am ready to invest the time, energy and money into it. Three weeks later, Joe handed me an envelope at the end of the workday. He told me, "Do not open this until you get home." Upon arriving at home, I opened the envelope to find a letter. The letter said, "I researched the cost of one year at the local community college here is the money for you. You are WORTH the investment." That is all that it took to get my life into gear and head off to college. The Summer of 2005 I left my job, enrolled full-time in college and never looked back. What started out with a simple goal of an associate's degree has turned into a master's degree all because of one random act of kindness.

After graduating from college and beginning a full-time career I tried many times to repay Joe for his investment. He would always tell me "No, I will not let you do that all I ask for is your friendship and always remember you are worth the investment." Joe passed away in 2023. His desire to invest in his friends or someone in the community will never be forgotten. Joe honestly pushed me into my educational and career pathway because he invested time, energy and money into someone that he had no affiliation or connection to beyond a happen chance conversation he overheard at just the right time.

The Father-in-law

It is not every day that you get the opportunity to have such great character people in your life. As a floundering twenty-something young adult trying to learn the ropes of becoming an adult, enter Doug Smith (my future father-in-law). I truly believe in the reality that people will enter your life at just the right time. Maybe for a season or maybe for a lifetime. Sadly, we lost Doug in August of 2024 but his impact on my life, the lessons I learned from him, will forever be carried forward as I pass things on to his grandchildren.

It was an honor to be asked to speak at his funeral and the words I used there are the words I will use here to set the stage for Doug.

For 20 years I was gifted the opportunity to know Doug. Truthfully, I was intimidated by him at first having heard stories of the man nicknamed "Big Country". Having heard these numerous stories, one would think that he was a tall tale on the scale of Paul Bunyan and his Blue Ox. I kid you not I envisioned that I would be meeting a Sequoia Tree of a man tall/rooted.

Then I met him. He wasn't quite as scary as I had built him up in my mind to be. He was just a simple man. Welcoming, not too warm but was willing to give you the chance to make an impression on him. Oddly enough he wanted to talk about me playing football. Just a little odd for me but at the same time it allowed the opportunity to break the ice on things while I waited on his daughter.

While my first impression was that he was no Sequoia, I would later learn that he was loud like a lion, tough as nails and firm as his handshake, his presence filled the room while commanding respect among those graced by his presence. While Doug was all these tough, rigid descriptive things; what really got me over the years was that underneath this Blue-Collar Persona was a huge teddy bear. He was a man filled with love for family and friends like none other. The man who at 67 years of age still referred to his father as "daddy", the man that slowly lost his macho outer shell enough to laugh at the fact that his son-in-law finally gave him a kiss on the cheek, and he didn't get mad about it.

Doug was always willing to help others with anything. Here was the thing though you had to ask him. He would offer his assistance but would never overstep the boundary of helping until he was asked directly. I recall early in my marriage, that I always would ask my father for help with things. Sometimes, however, my dad was not always available to help due to farming and work obligations. Doug, always told me "I will help you." I would feel guilty using his assistance though as I felt that was a role for my father. However, once I got over the feeling of cheating on my father by asking my father-in-law for help in times of need, Doug was always ready to fill the role of whatever I needed of him in the moment. It may have been as simple as helping me move something around the house to more daunting tasks like moving the whole house when we moved, building not one but two fences for the dogs, tearing up a whole yard and resowing it so that I had the nicest yard in the neighborhood. There was absolutely nothing that he would not do for me.

While Doug did so many things to help me along life's journey the one thing that made me most proud of him was watching his servant's heart transform over 20 years. While Doug was always willing to go the extra mile for his friends and neighbors, it was his service to God over the last decade that will always be etched into my memory. For clarity purposes, Doug was a believer and held fast to his Christian upbringing. He was never asked to serve. He always was there to give his time at church. All that changed, when his daughter and I volunteered to help with Vacation Bible School one summer. I will never forget, Doug letting us know that he was going to drive the church van to ensure children could attend. He told me, "I told them I would drive the van for Bible School. If you can volunteer to teach classes, I can volunteer to help too." I may have never taught Doug anything in this life, but I like to think that I was able to help catapult his desire to serve in the church setting. Doug later went on to help with the Benevolence Fund, became a member of the Board of Trustees and one of his greatest titles was when he became a Deacon for the church. During his years of retirement that man probably spent more time serving within the church where needed than his typical forty-hour work week.

While we lost Doug his memory and impact is one of legends that will be talked about for years to come. He truly was one in a million, a tall tale of a man. Gone but never forgotten.

My Father

From birth I watched servanthood from my father. I must say that my father is one of a kind. He has impacted so many individuals. Yet, he doesn't realize the actual impact he has had in this life. From providing a helping hand, listening, offering advice, going as far as to lend money with no intention to collect. I have watched from a distance what it means to serve others. As I gain more wisdom, I realize the impact my father had. When my parents divorced, I was afforded the opportunity to live with my father. While some would say that is great, congrats. It cannot go unsaid my father gave up a career in construction to return home to assist in raising me and my sister, while also coming home to take over the family farm to ensure its proper operation. Many would say, "that is what a father does". While not incorrect, it was a choice. Deciding to leave a lucrative career to rear children and take over a floundering farm may not be everyone's greatest accomplishment in life but in my eyes my father set the standard. One decision ingrained the ideology of fatherhood and set forth the way I would serve my children later in life.

Maybe leaving a job is not enough for some. Let me share another story. As a child maybe eight years old, I recall a memory with my dad and sister. My sister, who is older than I am was joking with my dad about a pair of old sneakers he had. She made mention about how they were worn, cracked, the white leather was darkened from the wear. I will never forget my dad's response, he asked us "do you know why I wear these old shoes?" Stumped, I stated "no." He said, "I wear old shoes, so you do not go without." To this day that statement has stuck with me. As a child it caught me off guard. To this day, it is quite possibly one of the most profound statements to cross my ears. While I reminisced that conversation with him several times, that shaped me into the father I am today, ensuring I serve my children first, before taking care of myself.

One last story that must be shared. There is an old saying that "everything happens for a reason" I am a true believer in that. Following in my father's footsteps, earlier in 2024, I accepted a job with his former employer. While working there my goal was to ensure serving the people via coaching, motivational acts/ words and empowering individuals. One day a person wanted to come and speak with me about life in general. While they walked away from the meeting happier, I was left sitting in my office in silence, chill bumps on my arm and a heart that was beating fast. Upon leaving work that day I immediately called my sister. I said, "you are not going to believe this, our father indirectly saved someone's life, and I doubt he even knows it." My heart overflowing from what I had just heard, I knew that I would need to share the story with him at some point. I went to my father a few days later to let him know of the news. I said, "are you aware you saved someone's life?" I told the story that was shared with me. My father looked at me and said, "I had no idea." Another indirect lesson of servanthood from my father. A simple reminder that being a servant does not require money, oftentimes it is simply providing a patient ear, time, an encouraging word or a smile.

I hope that through these brief snippets of servanthood, I have impressed upon you that servanthood can come from those closest to us and from those that we had a rare chance encounter with. The four people I wrote about above transformed my life in so many ways. From childhood to adulthood each leaned into me to make me a better son, brother, father, and friend. Without these rare individuals placed in my life from birth until now I would most likely be drifting through life with no self-worth, no charted pathway forward. I ask of you to not be selfish with your gifts and talents, but be like my Granny, Joe, Doug and my father and serve others more than you serve yourself. You will never know how much you can impact someone's life by just being selfless. To serve or be served the decision is up to you. I only hope that you will always choose servanthood at the end of the day as you will never know the legacy you will leave behind for others to continue telling others about the life you lived and the contributions you made upon this Earth while you graced it.

Servant Leadership Reflections

1. Reflect on a time when someone's act of servanthood deeply affected your life. What did you learn from that experience?

2. How can you incorporate acts of service into your daily routine?

3. Think about a role model who embodies the spirit of servanthood. What qualities do they possess that inspire you?

4. Consider the legacy you want to leave behind. How can servanthood be a part of that legacy?

5. In what ways can you encourage others in your community to embrace servanthood?

AUTHOR BIOGRAPHY
Garrett Milby

With over a decade of experience, my professional journey is rooted in diverse roles that highlight a strong commitment to education and leadership. At Dart Container Corporation, I served as a Senior Trainer, where I led training programs for over 1200 manufacturing employees. This initiative dramatically reduced turnover rates and enhanced productivity within the company, illustrating the power of effective training and development.

In my role as a Military Partnership Executive at Indiana Wesleyan University, I focused on building robust enrollment pipelines, engaging in extensive outreach to connect military personnel with educational opportunities. My work in this area demonstrated the importance of strategic partnerships and community engagement in driving institutional growth.

My admissions expertise is further enriched by my work at Lincoln College of Technology, where I played a pivotal role in guiding students toward fulfilling educational paths. This experience underscored my dedication to helping individuals achieve their career aspirations through education.

As a Master Sergeant with the Kentucky Air National Guard, I provided essential support with a focus on compliance and career development. This role demanded strong leadership skills and a commitment to nurturing the growth of those under my command.

Armed with advanced degrees in Organizational Leadership (MA) and Workforce Leadership (BS), as well as certifications such as John Maxwell Coach, my professional approach combines strategic leadership with transformative educational practices.

Garrett Milby
milbyg@hotmail.com
502-931-2679

SERVANT LEADERSHIP IN EDUCATION

By Karen Storey

SERVANT LEADERSHIP IN EDUCATION

What is a servant leader?

According to Webster's dictionary, leadership is "the capacity to guide the actions of a person or group of people." To be a servant one must be a follower or a disciple, "one who follows the opinions or teachings of another".

These two words seem to be contradictory and even oppositional to each other, yet Jesus was the greatest servant leader who has ever lived. In Matthew's Gospel, Chapter 4, Jesus calls his first disciples, (verses 18-22) and they immediately follow him. In verses 22-25 we see crowds of people beginning to follow Jesus. Why did they do this? What propelled them to exert their time and energy to pursue such a person? Jesus was not considered "one of the religious or community leaders". Matthew, Chapter 5 tells us that Jesus saw the crowds and taught them. This chapter is known as "The Beatitudes, or Sermon on the Mount". Yet in this same chapter, verse 17, we read that Jesus was a follower of the "Law of the Prophets."

Steps to becoming a servant leader

So, how do we become a servant leader?

First, we must become a student, "an attentive and systematic observer" of what we want to teach or share with others. We cannot lead someone if we are unskilled in what we are teaching. It would be as if someone wanting to be a firefighter rushed into a raging burning building without knowing what to do. We must first learn all that we can and master the material. This is what Jesus did when he studied the "Law of the Prophets", according to the Gospel of Luke, Chapter 2, verses 41-49.

Second, we must have a very clear vision of what we want to accomplish. This must be an "all-in" commitment, without any doubts. It is the core of who we are and what we are all about. We must be completely determined in our resolution to accomplish this goal, no backing down or giving up is allowed. We are told in the Gospels that Christ lived what he taught.

Third, we must begin to gather a group of like-minded people that will champion and support our vision and mission. As you share your story people will begin to gather around you to listen and support your efforts. Over time, as you speak your truth and share your core self, crowds will gather to learn more about your mission. Again, the Gospels pose significant and intimate details of how Jesus shared his message of love and forgiveness for ALL people.

Fourth, we must give back to our group though support, acceptance, kindness, gratitude, appreciation, honesty, mercy, hope, faith, peace, and love. All through the Gospels we are shown that Jesus did these things on a continual basis.

Fifth, we must inspire, motivate, and equip our followers **AND** give them the authority to begin and follow through on the mission to reach out to others and show them/teach them how to do what we have shown/ taught them. Teaching them how and why is an ongoing process. As servant leaders the support we give our team is perhaps the most difficult and important because it is not a "one time and done" process. Support is an ongoing process. It requires commitment and continual understanding, kindness, forgiveness, and leadership of/for your followers.

Two examples of Servant Leadership

When I was an Environmental Science teacher at Reagan High School here in Winston-Salem, North Carolina one of my seniors approached me about starting the Reagan Environmental Club. As a senior, Lee had a lot on her plate; applying to colleges, finishing her senior year, planning where she would be next year and what she would study… Yet she gave her time, energy and efforts to establish this club and recruit other like-minded students to embrace taking the campus "green" through setting up the guidelines of the club, talking to various businesses about her mission, having weekly meetings with myself (her sponsor), the school principal, various advisors, and then other students. She had to disseminate information, advertise, and recruit other students and supporters to join her mission. This club grew into a mighty force that affected all of Winston-Salem. During this time Winston-Salem put a ban on smoking in ALL public buildings, which was a huge endeavor, as we are the birthplace of tobacco growth and production (Reynolds Tobacco, RJR). Through Lee's initiative, this club began to inspire other students to grow in other sectors of our community. One student from our group attended Centenary United Methodist Church and she began a "Love Thy Neighbor" campaign that fed the homeless population once a month on the side lawn of the church. This practice continues to this day. From the vision and mission of ONE high school senior her vision for our community, as an "environmentally sustainable community", continues and has many followers. She chose to serve, gathered others around her, honored and supported those who followed her lead and never gave up on her mission.

During a trip to Washington DC, I met Bob, a leader of the National Association of Realtor's educational sector and a leader in public education. He told me that if I really wanted to impact students' lives, I needed to teach middle school, because by the time a child reaches high school it is almost too late... So, I took a position at Wiley Middle School, as an 8th grade science teacher. One unit in the 8th grade science curriculum is Environmental Science. During my 2nd year at Wiley, I had two students, Madison and Holly, who took the lead to begin the "Wiley Go Green Club". The campus is downtown and was in desperate need of clearing overgrowth, trash and litter. Also, there were no recycling efforts established for this school or for any school in Winston Salem/Forsyth County. They ask me to be their sponsor, and I happily agreed. They wrote the documents needed to set up the club and met with the principal. The principal agreed and the club was born. Madison and Holly presented their idea to the team of students, asked for class time to implement their campus cleanup efforts, and spent many hours after school working on their mission with other students and teachers. At the end of the year the school was recognized by the county for their beautification efforts and their recycling campaign. The Women's Garden Club also supported and recognized these two students for their leadership and the city of Raleigh gave azaleas to be planted at the school in recognition of their outstanding accomplishments. Recycling of all schools in Winston Salem/Forsyth County continues to this day and beautification efforts are a part of every school.

Summary of Servant Leadership

We see examples every day of people who, when a need presents itself, have the expertise, a vision, a purpose, a mission and the determination to fill that need. These are people who have studied the subject matter, become experts in the subject and then begin to gather a group of like-minded people with determination and commitment. Here in North Carolina, Hurricane Helene devastated many of our Western counties, and many people have come together and taken their time, energy and resources to meet the needs of those affected. They did not wait for FEMA, or other government agencies to decide what to do…they immediately jumped into action and begin to take the initiative to reach out and ask for the support of others that could help relieve the suffering of those impacted by the hurricane.

A servant leader can be **<u>any given age and can show up at any time</u>**. They will always face many challenges, as life is filled with unexpected twists and turns. Yet, the servant leader persists in his/her mission because their vision is ever before them and their determination is unbreakable. Knowing they alone cannot accomplish the mission, a servant leader spends their time, energy and resources to gather like-minded people to help fulfill the mission. A servant leader must **NEVER** forget to support their team and recognize it is the teamwork of everyone involved that has contributed to the success of the mission. The servant leader has a huge responsibility upon their shoulders as this is a life-long journey. It is not for the "faint of heart" as it will demand determination, resilience, faith, hope, kindness, gratitude, compassion, acceptance, honesty, mercy, humility, and much more.

May you <u>be</u> empowered to <u>be</u>come the servant leader God wants you to <u>be</u>!

Servant Leadership Reflections

1. What is a cause or mission you feel passionate about? How can you begin to lead within this area?

   _____
   _____
   _____
   _____
   _____
   _____
   _____
   _____
   _____

2. Reflect on a time you followed or supported someone's leadership. What qualities made them an effective leader?

   _____
   _____
   _____
   _____
   _____
   _____
   _____
   _____
   _____

3. Consider your skills and knowledge. How can they contribute to a leadership role in your community?

_____
_____
_____
_____
_____
_____
_____
_____

4. Visualize gathering a community around your mission. What steps can you take to invite others to join your cause?

_____
_____
_____
_____
_____
_____
_____
_____
_____

5. How do you balance leading with serving in your current roles? What improvements can you make?

_____
_____
_____
_____
_____
_____
_____
_____
_____
_____

AUTHOR BIOGRAPHY
Karen Storey

Karen Storey is a power house of knowledge, resources, and inspiration when it comes to "GOING GREEN" and "BUILDING THRIVING COMMUNITY PARTNERSHIPS". Karen comes from a strong background of more than 30 years' experience in advertising sales, marketing, teaching, and business coaching, coupled with a Master's Degree in Curriculum and Instruction from Virginia Tech, and a certification in Gifted Education from High Point University.

As an environmental educator Karen is on a personal mission to build, support, sustain, and grow thriving local communities that are supported by a strong Real Estate market and equally strong Education System.

Karen graduated Princeton High School at age 16 in the top 1 % of her class and went on to become an educator and business coach. During the 2006-2007 school year, she encouraged and facilitated 144 students at Ronald Reagan High School in Forsyth County, Winston-Salem, NC to volunteer more than 4,000 hours of community service with the goal of "connecting and sustaining our community and our world". In 2009 Karen Storey also sponsored and founded the Wiley Middle School" GO GREEN" Club.

Karen Storey truly believes that all individuals are connected and the Real Estate market influences the growth of a local community. Karen is committed to "stitching" our real estate, business, and educational community together in a comprehensive and cohesive environmentally sustainable "green" society.

Karen Storey served as Subject Matter Expert for the NAR GREEN Designation and is also a Keynote Speaker on "How to Become the Green Voice of Real Estate" in your local community. Additional NAR courses that Karen holds her designations and certifications and is passionate about teaching are the Accredited Buyer Representative (ABR), Resort and Second Property Specialist (RSPS), and Senior Real Estate Specialist (SRES).

Karen's Mission: Passionate to help others achieve "the next level" in their business to produce measurable, positive, long lasting results. Believe that life is a "win-win" for ALL, when built on a solid foundation of respect, integrity, and accountability. We are no longer a "self-sufficient" community, but are interconnected in a global market place. Each local community leaves its ecological and carbon footprint which identifies its "grassroots" effort in the global market. It is crucial we support each other within our community, and in return providing a cohesive environmentally sustainable global market place. When we do this everyone wins!

IN THE EYE OF THE STORM: A JOURNEY OF SERVANT LEADERSHIP

By Tricia Andreassen

IN THE EYE OF THE STORM: A JOURNEY OF SERVANT LEADERSHIP

September 29, 2024, is a day that remains vivid in my heart, one etched into the stories of those living along the east coast and in the tranquil mountain areas of Georgia, South Carolina, North Carolina, and Tennessee. It was the day Hurricane Helene barged into our lives with such force that it left us all a in overwhelm and shock. That morning, as Kurt and I sat together at our kitchen table, sorting out the flow of our master class, I casually mentioned, "The storm's looking fierce—we might need more bottled water and basics." Kurt shrugged with his usual calm, "We're fine with what we've got." Yet, deep down, a little voice nudged me—insisting we make that run. So, off we went, Kurt by my side, like always. It was part of our routine, really; we'd seen enough hyped-up weather reports that fizzled into nothing. But Helene wasn't like the rest.

Returning home, our phones exploded with a tornado alert—it demanded immediate action. We gathered in the bathroom while the alarms were going off. When the skies seemed to ease a little, Kurt reached out to Amanda, a dear friend tucked away in the mountains near our cabin. We needed to know she was okay, especially with the flood warnings growing louder. Her reply came with a dose of humor, "For water to flood my hill, it'd have to be Biblical."

But slowly, as the day unfurled, we learned Helene wasn't just passing through—she was here to stay. Darkness enveloped the grid, calls cut off, the digital chatter ceased. It was a chilling silence, signaling the storm's wrath. Our son, Jordan, came over to stay with us since he was without power. Since we lived an hour and a half from our mountain home, we didn't realize what might be happening. Our home was experiencing power outages and trees down but that didn't even come close to what was happening near our second home. To some, it's just an Airbnb, but to me and Kurt, it's a cherished escape representing his Danish culture and my five generations of Appalachian living—a place blessed with the quiet whispers of Newland, North Carolina that is my special place where I feel at peace and close to God.

Beyond the swirling storm tales and wreckage, lies a story less told—the rise of profound leadership in midst of a life-taking storm that will take years to recover from. People were not driven by personal agendas or the quest for accolades, but by an innate urge to help, and to survive together. As chaos reigned, individuals emerged with the heart of servant leaders, especially in Helene's aftermath, where the sense of community and generosity shone brilliantly amid the ruin. Even though it's been months since this storm, our communities will be in great need for years to come.

Over the years, in my writings about leadership, I've come across many who don't see themselves as leaders. Undeniably, they are the silent heroes, like Crystal, who devoted over a month to the Green Valley Firehouse, devoting herself to organizing much-needed supplies without any desire for recognition. In her tireless spirit, true leadership manifested itself—in those moments when others might waver. Stories of firefighters tirelessly guiding campers to safety, contrasted with the grim fates of those who hesitated and lost their lives.

Among these stories of loss are countless unsung stories of kindness—people offering food, shelter, financial help, and their time to lift others. These accounts are more than heartwarming; they're transformative, stirring a reflection on leadership as a call to serve. The quiet doers—those knitting blankets, raising funds, connecting people together and searching for others—embody the essence of "it takes a village," turning the saying into reality.

I find an abundance of love and hope in knowing that true leadership is about giving freely, without expecting reward. It's about unity during daunting times, showcasing the human spirit's boundless resilience and its profound capacity to inspire others.

In the aftermath of a natural disaster, where chaos and devastation dominate, leaders face a crucial test of character and purpose. As servant leaders we are called to step forward with an outstretched hand, rather than an upraised one. We are also called to lead ourselves; act, no matter how small it may seem. In the past I would have been able to walk among the rubble and help with "boots on the ground" action. I could have worked tirelessly serving food to long lines of people at a community center. However, in dealing with a chronic pain illness I had to process differently and reflect on how I could help. It was in the process of gathering food to drop off, do videos to share where to go for food, paint angels and give them to people in need and ask my connections to give in different ways.

The Power of Compassion in Leadership

Kurt and I stopped into a store in Spruce Pine, North Carolina that has been in business for generations. The owner shared with us how her parents owned the business before her and operated it as a florist. During conversation, we gathered our hands together and prayed for the community and those who lost so much. One story that has stayed dominant on me was an eight-year-old little girl who lost both of her parents in the flood. As she lives with her grandparents and the church continues to help their family, I close my eyes and visualize this little girl when she is older. I want her to remember the power of community, the strength of faith and the compassion she was shown. When I think of this, it causes me to stay committed in the practice of servant leadership. There is a saying that people won't remember what you say but will remember how you make them feel. Sometimes the initial response often focuses on assessing damage and mobilizing resources. However, true servant leaders know that compassion must guide our actions. It's not always what we say or give in quantities of something but instead understand the emotions and needs of those affected, allowing leaders to tailor their responses to uplift communities effectively. The little things such as a greeting card, a letter, or a painted rock can be so powerful that it creates transformation where it's needed.

It's through organized relief efforts; leaders exemplify compassion by integrating empathy and understanding into their actions. To create long term healing and restoration, leaders must be willing to serve long after a natural disaster like Helene. Leaders can promote these values through actions like volunteering time, sharing resources generously, or advocating community resilience and growth. Imagine the impact we could have introducing these studies and principles into schools so that children can learn servant leadership from a young age. That is my hope and prayer as one who lives to serve and inspire.

Igniting the Flame of Hope

In the heart of servant leadership lies the role of inspiring others to act and believe in the possibility of growth and recovery. As a leader grounded in my purpose-driven faith, I am continuously reminded of the power of the grain of a mustard seed can provide as a beacon of hope and motivation. Inspiration doesn't solely arise from grand speeches or declarations; it flourishes through living examples of resilience and unwavering faith.

"For truly I tell you, if you have faith the size of a mustard seed, move from here to there' and it will move; and nothing will be impossible for you." Matthew 17:20-21

It's about doing our best to show up every day with a spirit that encourages others to rise and join the journey towards recovery and renewal. Of course, we are human and there are days we are going to struggle. This is why servant leadership works. It becomes powerful when we join, share our vulnerability and lift one another in time of need. When we give and then allow for others to give to us a spark becomes a flame, and that flame fuels the hearts of everyone.

You Can Serve Right Now

If you have it in your heart to contribute to the families that have been impacted by Hurricane Helene in Western North Carolina please consider Samaritan's Purse at SamaritansPurse.org and also BePreparedBeReady.org where I am on the Board of Directors which helps families impacted through crisis. Currently we are preparing Kits for Kids that educate children on how to handle themselves during disaster situations as well as their parents. This encourages communication between the child and the parent on how to become better prepared when a crisis comes. The actual "KitsForKids" includes a tracker, a recording from their parents to help them stay calm if they are separated from them and reminders of what steps to take. It also includes a tourniquet, Mylar blanket/poncho, whistle, light and emergency contact information. The foundation is also preparing these for elderly, pets and those with disabilities. During an emergency such as what we experienced in our area, the go bag can be a full emergency kit. Our hope is to educate as many people as possible on what to do then faced with disasters in their community. Coni Meyers, my Co-Author in this book is the founder of this incredible non-profit to raise awareness about sustainability and disaster preparedness.

AUTHOR BIOGRAPHY
Tricia Andreassen

AS SEEN ON:

From a young age, Tricia Andreassen knew her calling was to inspire and bring hope to audiences worldwide as a speaker and singer. At just 19 years old, she became an entrepreneur by purchasing her first real estate property with no money in her pocket, growing up in a trailer. Her passion for business ignited when she took her first Marketing and Economics classes and becoming an assistant for a real estate broker while being mentored from a prominent attorney. After the tragic loss of a close friend in a car accident, Tricia channeled her grief into writing a heartfelt story of hope, which she sent to the grieving mother. Encouraged by her English professor, who mentored her writing, Tricia began to align her talents and life purpose.

If you have ever felt you were meant for more in your life and believe that your business and personal purpose can harmoniously blend, Tricia's message is for you. Or, if you've already built your business and grown your influence. Now, it's time to share that expertise with the world.

With over 30 years of experience, Tricia Andreassen has mastered the art of transforming knowledge into powerful, impactful communication. She has shared the stage with influential figures such as Tony Robbins, NY Times Best Selling Author and Speaker John Maxwell, Piers Morgan, NY Times Best Selling Author Jon Gordon, NY Times Best Selling Author Malcolm Gladwell and Dr. Oz.

Tricia genuinely cares about empowering others. Her mission is to help you uncover and amplify your unique talents and strengths, turning them into unstoppable momentum. Whether you're ready to become a keynote speaker, craft a bestselling book, or coauthor with top-tier thought leaders, Tricia is dedicated to helping you leverage your expertise and elevate your brand.

How Tricia Can Help You:

1. **Speak on Stages:** Become a sought-after speaker who captivates audiences with a universally resonant message. Tricia will coach you on crafting your signature

talk, refining your delivery, and present with unstoppable confidence to secure speaking opportunities that amplify your voice and impact.

2. **Teach and Train:** Your knowledge and experience are meant to be shared. Learn to create proprietary products for passive income that you can sell repeatedly, extending your reach and influence.

3. **Write Your Book:** Whether it's your first book or your next bestselling project, Tricia will guide you through the writing process. She will help turn your expertise into a tangible product that establishes you as a leader in your field.

4. **Collaborate with Elite Leaders:** Imagine coauthoring a book with high caliber thought leaders. This collaboration can exponentially grow your reach and expose you to new audiences. Tricia offers rare opportunities to a select group of leaders to coauthor alongside her, enhancing their brand, exposure, credibility, and media opportunities.

5. **Provide You A Custom Marketing and Media Roadmap:** Tricia has become an Authority in her field providing a high-level view of one's marketing strategy from brand story and messaging to offline presentation such as elevator pitch and in-person presentation to online presence such as online website with lead generation and elements that include how to develop a plan to present yourself on stages, podcasts, YouTube and other channels as well as how to create multiple streams of income such as courses, memberships, and polished keynotes and presentations that pulls all of your business

vision all together with one coach and one solution. Imagine having a coach that understands everything you want to accomplish.

Tricia's work has been featured on platforms like Dr. Oz, Faith Unveiled Network, 700 Club, UplifTV, FOX, NBC, and CBS as well as backstage in speaking with licensing coaching for Dr. Phil, Good Morning America, 20/20. Her creative and entrepreneurial legacy is a unique blend of practical business insights and artistic innovation. Tricia is also a singer and a fine artist, with her work displayed in galleries across the U.S.

Why wait? It's time to step onto the stage, write your book, and share your message with the world. Visit **www.TriciaAndreassen.com** to learn more her speaking, CreateCoreU.com to learn about her AI Marketing and Coaching University. Go to LiveLifeUnstoppable.com for information on her coaching, training, and personal mission of her purpose and get her FREE eBook and trainings.

www.ingramcontent.com/pod-product-compliance
Lightning Source LLC
Chambersburg PA
CBHW070103080526
44586CB00013B/1168